PRAISE FOR

HAPPILY GENEROUS

"Happily Generous is an extraordinary, life-changing book, a perfect example of what happens when deep faith, hard-earned wisdom, a gentle spirit, and epic writing chops all merge. Mike Kocolowski has given us a priceless gift that will lead many to a priceless life."

—**MARK ATTEBERRY**, AWARD-WINNING AUTHOR OF *THE SAMSON SYNDROME*

"What a joy! Mike Kocolowski has written a real page-turner. *Happily Generous* is packed with fresh stories, biblical truths, and personal insights that affirm my lifelong belief in the power of generosity. Be generous to yourself and read this priceless book. You will be blessed!"

—**PAT WILLIAMS**, CO-FOUNDER OF THE ORLANDO MAGIC AND AUTHOR OF *LEADERSHIP EXCELLENCE*

"This book masterfully tackles the most essential yet least understood and practiced facet of the Christian faith: generosity. It's beautifully written and theologically sound, with personal anecdotes to help you gain a much-needed perspective. If you let it, it will challenge and stretch you in all the right ways and will surely become a favorite you will come back to again and again."

—**LEO SABO**, PRESIDENT OF CHRISTIAN STEWARDSHIP NETWORK

"Mike's stories and insights on God's purpose for your life are inspirational. They will touch your heart and challenge you to think. Read this book and learn how you can be a generosity artist. God is calling us to be like him, happily generous."

—**D. CLAY PERKINS, PH.D.**, EXECUTIVE VICE PRESIDENT OF FINANCIAL PLANNING MINISTRY

"I love this book! Mike Kocolowski gives the reader a ride through history. Generosity as seen through his personal and leadership life. *Happily Generous* will change your life—and if lived correctly—millions of others as well."

—**JOE PUTTING**, SENIOR PASTOR OF TOMOKA CHRISTIAN CHURCH AND AUTHOR OF *WE SAID YES*

"This book ties together the thread of abundant generosity that is woven throughout the entire Bible. It is countercultural to believe we will not find fulfillment in buying more toys, obtaining more power, and living a lifestyle of comfort and security. But it truly is more blessed to give than receive, and the better life is the life marked with joyful generosity. Mike does a great job using Scripture and personal stories to show us that true happiness, freedom, and peace come from living a happily generous life. Everything in our possession is a gift from God and is to be joyfully stewarded by us for His glory! Jesus showed us how to live generously with delight; now He asks us to do likewise. Read this book, let it sink in, and live it."

—**JEFF SHARDA**, LEAD PASTOR OF FINANCE & OPERATIONS AT HARVEST BIBLE CHAPEL

"Mike Kocolowski is the Chief Stewardship Officer of Christian Financial Resources and one of my trusted stewardship advisors. He has helped countless partner ministries unleash generosity with his wise counsel. I cannot wait to hear the stories of people taking further steps in their generosity journey after reading this book!"

—**DARREN KEY**, CEO OF CHRISTIAN FINANCIAL RESOURCES AND AUTHOR OF *THE QUEST*

"The problem with most books on generosity is that only generous people enjoy reading them. But my friend Mike has penned one that will pull you in, both head and heart, even if you have doubts about the generous life. In our best moments, we want to be generous, but for many of us, the train never leaves the station. You've found a book that will help you realize why it's in your best interest to become a person who lives to give. Read it. And never look back."

—**EDDIE LOWEN**, LEAD PASTOR OF WESTSIDE CHRISTIAN CHURCH

"Mike has a generous heart and he captures the essence of a generous heart in *Happily Generous*. The book is both practical and inspirational. It would be a great gift for teaching people to be generous and to help those who already give to grow in their generosity and happiness. If I were still leading a church, I would want to put this in the hands of every member."

—**MIKE WAERS**, DIRECTOR OF CHURCH RELATIONS AT POINT UNIVERSITY

"I was gripped with gratitude while reading this book. It's delightful and insightful, personal and profound, meaningful and motivating. While I've long known Mike professionally, I now feel that I know him personally. Author Chip Ingram said, 'The Bible teaches us that generosity is a gateway to intimacy with God.' To that I would add, generosity is also a gateway to intimacy with others. In reading this book I'm compelled to live more generously in order to enjoy life with God and others more abundantly!"

—**DR. ALAN AHLGRIM**, CHIEF SOUL CARE OFFICER AT COVENANT CONNECTIONS AND AUTHOR OF *SOUL STRENGTH: RHYTHMS FOR THRIVING*

"In *Happily Generous*, Mike Kocolowski does a phenomenal job at making a compelling Biblical case for the necessity, and benefits, of generosity among God's people. His artful use of words keeps the reader engaged. The message will resonate with the life experience of everyone, as the truth tends to do. I found my personal experiences with giving reinforced, encouraged, and challenged. I have been blessed to know Mike for a few decades and I have personally seen the redemptive work of the Holy Spirit in his life that makes this wonderful book possible. It is written from a place of personal experience and growth and is truly a statement of God's powerful effect in the surrendered life."

—**DR. DAVID M. MCGREW, MD**, LEAD PHYSICIAN FOR FLORIDA AND GEORGIA, AND SENIOR LEADERSHIP INFLUENCER FOR INNOVATION AND INTEGRATION, AT CARELON HEALTHCARE

"In a world characterized by greed, Mike Kocolowski invites his readers to live with the type of generosity only possible by the grace of God. His invitation is rooted in the very character of God and the fact that we are made in the image of God. Mike urges us to set aside the many things that can't satisfy, embrace the gifts of God, and become givers of what we have received. When we do this, we can experience the happiness and abundant life that only God can provide."

—**STEPHEN WAERS**, PH.D., CHIEF ACADEMIC OFFICER OF POINT UNIVERSITY

"When I think of Mike Kocolowski, two words immediately come to mind: faithfulness and wisdom. All of us, in our quest for a better life, opt out of some of the practices that actually lead us to it. Mike helps us with that. He escorts us down a path to the life we all want. Take the happily generous journey. Let him be your trail guide. You will be glad you did!"

—**GREG LINDSEY**, LEAD PASTOR OF DISCOVERY CHURCH, COLORADO, AND AUTHOR OF *THE REST OF YOUR STORY: THE PATH TO THE CHRISTIAN LIFE YOU WANT*

"Mike masterfully connects the dots and reveals the mystery between happiness and generosity! He excels in drawing from his own personal life experiences and illustrating the teachings rooted in scripture about giving and generosity. Indeed, generosity is embedded in our DNA. I love his 'two-minute experiment that can last the rest of your life.' I highly recommend this book!"

—**ROGER SHEPHERD, MA, LMHC**, FOUNDER OF FLORIDA COUNSELING FOUNDATION AND SHEPHERD MINISTRIES AT THE LIGHTHOUSE

"Living generously as a follower of Christ can be expressed in so many different ways. I am thankful Mike has taken his time, talent, and treasure to generously bless all who read this book with practical and powerful Biblical wisdom to be able to live a generous life themselves. Mike reminds us all, not only through his writing but also his life, that what really matters are items of eternal significance, and one of the most significant things we can do out of our love for God is give as He did when He gave us the indescribable gift of His Son."

—**J. KEVIN INGRAM**, PRESIDENT OF MANHATTAN CHRISTIAN COLLEGE

"Happily Generous teaches us the best times in our life are not when we receive but when we give our time, our smiles, our hearts, and yes, our money. This book is a must read for anyone struggling with scarcity, living in fear, and holding tight to their resources. I was reminded that my happiest memories came from helping others in need, while I trusted Jesus to supply my daily needs."

—**JOHNNA REEDER KLEYMEYER**, PRESIDENT & CEO, COLORADO SPRINGS CHAMBER OF COMMERCE AND ECONOMIC DEVELOPMENT CORPORATION

HAPPILY GENEROUS

THE SECRET TO
LIVING A PRICELESS LIFE

MIKE KOCOLOWSKI

Helping talented writers
publish exceptional books.

HAPPILY GENEROUS

THE SECRET TO LIVING A PRICELESS LIFE

MIKE
KOCOLOWSKI

www.AcornPublishingLLC.com

For information, address:
Acorn Publishing, LLC
3943 Irvine Blvd. Ste. 218
Irvine, CA 92602

Happily Generous: The Secret to Living a Priceless Life
Copyright © 2024 Mike Kocolowski

Cover design by Damonza.com
Interior design and formatting by Debra Cranfield Kennedy

Printed in the United States of America

ISBN-13: 979-8-88528-098-3 (hardcover)
ISBN-13: 979-8-88528-097-6 (paperback)
Library of Congress Control Number (LCCN): 2024905223

♦ ♦ ♦

To my wife, Mary Ann.

When our eyes first met in that tenth-grade biology class,

I felt the chemistry.

As they say, the rest is history.

You're still the best thing that has ever happened to me.

CONTENTS

CONTENTS

INTRODUCTION

◆ ◆ ◆

MORE BLESSED

All men seek happiness. This is without exception.

BLAISE PASCAL

It is more blessed to give than to receive.

JESUS

*M*y most memorable childhood Christmas began like all the others. Well before dawn, one of the five kids in my family would wake up, leap out of bed, and rouse the others with an eager whisper: *It's Christmas! Let's go look at our presents!* We'd tinker around under the tree, sorting wrapped gifts, searching for labels bearing our names.

"Michael, that's yours!"

"Johnny, you got one too!"

"This tag says 'Theresa'!"

"Here's a present for Cathi and one for Laura ... looks like the same thing."

Eventually, one of us led the parade into our parents' bedroom to coax them from their slumber. A few gentle pushes, little voices pleading, then five of us piling onto their bed. The piling-on always did the trick. We had them outnumbered. They couldn't pretend to still be asleep.

As a family of modest means, each child normally unwrapped four or five inexpensive gifts on Christmas. A few practical items like clothing—often mom-made knitted hats, scarves, and gloves for the icy Chicago winter—and a couple of toys.

But this Christmas was different. All the gifts were store-bought. And stacked higher than a skyscraper! Presents and joy filled our living room! I don't recall every gift opened that morning, but I'll never forget the pair of three-speed bicycles—one for the boys to share and one for the girls—standing there with a bow on each seat. Those Free Spirit bikes from Sears topped off the banner harvest.

What a Christmas it was! Five delighted children. And two parents . . . even *happier*.

A line in red letters appears in the Bible late in the book of Acts: *"It is more blessed to give than to receive"* (Acts 20:35). Or as Eugene Peterson phrases it, *"You're far happier giving than getting."* Skeptics may scoff and doubters may doubt, but on that Christmas morning my parents felt the truth of that statement. Surely, on occasion at least, you have as well. The question is: Do you want to experience it more?

Everyone wants to be happy. Most people want to be generous. But few appreciate the mysterious connection between the two pursuits. You might even say the road to happiness is paved with generosity. Can you imagine it?

Your destination is happiness and a thousand roads clamor for your attention claiming to show the way to the hidden treasure. "Come this way," shouts Materialism. "Over here," says Popularity. "This is the path for you," promises Power. Bombarded by 10,000 ads per day; enticed by ego-building attention and recognition; attracted to control, authority, and a platform for influence, it's no wonder we nip at the bait the world dangles.

Meanwhile, a less-traveled road, a narrow road, a road without flashing signs and neon lights sits lonely, waiting for company. Will you dare step toward this trail? It offers an upside-down, inside-out, last-shall-be-first experience. Instead of collecting, you'll be distributing. Not self-absorbed, but others-focused. You'll trade bondage for liberty, stress for satisfaction, a rat race for a stroll in the park. Imagine your journey lighter and your smile brighter.

Generosity is more than an act of giving something of value to a person, organization, or cause. The attitude prompting the gesture matters. That's why the Apostle Paul's comments on giving include the words, "For God loves a cheerful giver" (2 Cor. 9:7). To say this book is purely about generosity would miss the bullseye. It's about being *happily* generous. Not reluctantly generous. Not grudgingly generous. Not pridefully, showily, snobbishly generous. Of course, it's not a book focused only on happiness, either. Not happily selfish, happily successful, happily rich, or happily retired. Happily *generous*. The two ideas, happiness and generosity, join hands and marry. Together forever, they form the foundation of a priceless life.

Before we move on, a few clarifications and disclosures are in order.

IT'S NOT WRONG TO RECEIVE

Jesus never implied it was wrong to be on the receiving end of a generous gesture. He who washed the feet of his disciples on the night of his betrayal once allowed a woman to anoint his own feet with expensive perfume. Our Savior encourages us to ask, seek, knock, and promises to give, reveal, and open. Our heavenly father, the source and supplier of all we need, loves to shower us with blessings and always will. "Every good and perfect gift is from above, coming down from the Father of the heavenly lights, who does not change like shifting shadows" (James 1:17). He's delighted when we receive these gifts with gratitude.

Jesus simply made a comparison, "It is more blessed to give than to receive." Another way to say it is, "Receiving is wonderful, but giving is even better." Receiving is like a couple of nights relaxing at a local Ramada Inn. But giving is like an oceanside weekend at the Ritz Carlton. Or think of your favorite food. Chocolate? Pizza? Glazed donuts? A twelve-ounce medium-rare filet mignon served on a 500-degree plate? All very good, but something better exists. Melted chocolate, poured over a scoop of vanilla ice cream. Eating pizza, watching your favorite team win the Super Bowl. A box of glazed donuts, paired with a steaming mug of coffee. A perfectly cooked filet alongside green beans, a baked potato, and half a loaf of warm, buttered bread. You get the point. And now you're hungry. There's nothing wrong with receiving. It's good, actually. But giving feels deeper, fuller, more satisfying.

GENEROSITY IS EXPRESSED IN A VARIETY OF WAYS

Oftentimes when we think of generosity, our thoughts jump instantly to money. We tend to measure giving in dollars and cents. The Bible talks a lot about money and it will always be a big part of the generosity conversation, but generosity speaks many languages and displays itself in various ways: a cup of cold water, an hour of time, a kind word, a helping hand.

Imagine a person who faithfully gives ten percent (or more) of his or her income to worthy causes. Those dollars fight poverty, build libraries, spread the gospel, and heal the sick. But this person undertips the hardworking waitress, won't offer directions to a lost tourist, rarely has time for anyone, and never volunteers for anything. In other words, aside from their ritualistic financial contributions, they live daily life like a pre-converted Grinch. That's not the description of a generous person. And probably not a happy person either.

WE ALL HAVE ROOM TO GROW

Would you like to be less happy? Would you like to be less generous? Highly doubtful. Wherever you are in your generosity journey, this book is about taking your next best step.

You might feel guilty because today you give sparingly. Your budget is tight. Resources are scarce. The bills won't stop. The kids need braces, your car is a clunker, and college tuition lurks in the bushes. Forget about saving for retirement.

Perhaps you feel a speck of pride because you're in the circle of top givers in your church or community. Your large gift fed the hungry, housed the homeless, built a new children's wing, saved a nonprofit from going under.

It's possible you feel complacent because you've been tithing since you were two years old. You've religiously followed the principle you learned as a child and giving is as automatic as brushing your teeth.

Maybe you're nervous (or annoyed) about being challenged in a personal matter. This is between you and God and no one else, you think.

Or it could be that generosity is one-dimensional for you. You've never connected it to anything other than a transaction of cold, hard cash.

Regardless of the situation, we all have room to grow.

Do you want a different kind of abundance and lasting happiness? Henri Nouwen's words offer insight: "Our greatest fulfillment lies in giving ourselves to others. We become beautiful people when we give whatever we can give: a smile, a handshake, a kiss, an embrace, a word of love, a present, a part of our life ... all of our life."[1]

Are you ready to hike the happiness trail and discover God's dream for you?

As your guide and companion, the Counselor and Comforter will accompany you on this pilgrimage. The Holy Spirit stands packed and ready. Love, joy, and peace fill his pockets. Patience, kindness, and goodness cram his backpack. Gentleness, faithfulness, and self-control crowd his suitcase. He's well-supplied and open-handed—whatever you need will never run out.

It's early Christmas morning, two decades after those three-speed bicycles appeared in our living room. Now I'm the parent. Mary Ann and I hear our four children: Michele (8), Melanie (7), Melissa (4), and Matthew (2) whisper in the distance. It'll happen soon. They'll tiptoe into our bedroom. They'll poke, pounce, and pile on. Outnumbered, we won't stand a chance. The presents under the tree need unwrapping. Immediately!

The small voices, however, don't draw closer. Minutes pass. What's going on? Perhaps they recall the Christmas rule: "Don't wake us up until daylight." While we wonder what's delaying the blitz of eager children, the smell of bacon drifts into our bedroom. Eventually, eight little legs march in to "wake" us up. "Mom, Dad, we have a surprise for you! Close your eyes, take our hands, come with us." And a new Kocolowski family tradition begins.

The table is full. Two place settings with all the silverware. Bacon and eggs; juice and coffee; pancakes and sausage. English muffins, home fries, a bottle of ketchup—gotta have ketchup. While the budding Michelin-star chefs grin ear-to-ear, we savor a bona fide breakfast buffet. It beats the scoop of granola I usually eat each morning.

What a wonderful Christmas! Two delighted parents. And four children, even *happier*. The simple act of serving breakfast introduced them to the reality of Jesus' teaching: *It is more blessed to give than to receive.*

Have you tasted the truth of these curious words? Hungry for more?

Let's read on. Our journey beckons. A happier, more generous life awaits. And it's priceless!

CHAPTER ONE

• • •

THE GREAT GIVER

The measure of all love is its giving.
The measure of God's love is the cross of Christ.

J. I. PACKER

CHAPTER ONE

THE GREAT GIVER

*F*or God so loved the world he gave . . .

Your brain might auto-complete that phrase with the rest of the words from John 3:16, the famous verse declaring the ultimate expression of God's unbounded love. While that single statement encapsulates the *depth* of his affection, God displays the *breadth* of his affection in ways often overlooked. Because nothing is impossible for the King of kings and Lord of lords, the manifestations of his generosity are endless.

God spoke and created the universe out of nothing. He carved the Grand Canyon and sculpted the Himalayas. He planted rainforests and dried up deserts. He filled oceans and froze the North Pole. Because of him, eagles have wings, butterflies beauty, lions strength, and cheetahs speed.

But that's nothing when you consider God breathed into dust and formed mankind.

He's the God of fruit, fertility, and a thousand fortunes. The God of restoration, reformation, reconstruction, and reconciliation. He breaks down prison walls, builds up broken hearts, casts out demons, and conquers addictions. And did you know he resurrects the dead!?

He gives the lame legs, the blind sight, the sick health, and the poor wealth. He offers rest to the weary, peace to the worried, faith to the fearful, and hope to the hurting.

But what will he do for you? Glad you asked.

He'll separate the sea to bring you to safety.

He'll slay a giant to give you victory.

He'll supply grace to embrace you with comfort.

And he'll forgive your sins to grant you freedom.

You are living proof. God holds nothing good back from those he loves.

He is, after all, the Great Giver. The Life Giver. The Generous One. And we should note at this point and never forget it: No being is happier than God. John Piper writes:

> Can you imagine what it would be like if the God
> who ruled the world were not happy? What if
> God were given to grumbling and pouting and
> depression, like some Jack-in-the-beanstalk giant
> in the sky? What if God were frustrated and
> despondent and gloomy and discontented and
> dejected? . . . . I don't think so.[1]

We serve a happy God. An active God. A for-us, with-us God. Stories of his mighty power and ever-present involvement crowd the cosmos. To the father who always loves us, our well-being always matters. The first pages of the Bible expose this reality.

Inventors, architects, artists, and songwriters begin with an end in mind. A sense of calling inspires their actions and sets them into motion. These creative souls conceive life-altering gadgets, design aesthetically pleasing buildings, paint captivating landscapes, and write heart-touching lyrics with deep, soulful melodies. The fruits of their labor begin with seeds of purpose.

So too, with God. He didn't create the heavens and earth on a whim. Purpose inspired design. Father, Son, and Spirit formed a world where everything was good, for us to enjoy.

In the beginning there was nothing. God took six days to form the universe, then rested on the seventh. His intentions were executed to perfection and stamped with his seal of approval. He spoke light into existence. Same for sky, dry land, seas, plants, animals, and so on. It was good, good, good, good, good. On day six, God created mankind and surveyed all he had done. Now it wasn't just good. It was *very* good. Happy with his work and delighted to entrust a wondrous paradise to beings molded in his image, God also gave us a remarkable capacity to enjoy his marvelous creation. When he built this world, we were on his mind.

The profundity of it all leaves us speechless. It calls to mind the psalmist's contemplation, worded this way by Eugene Peterson:

I look up at your macro-skies, dark and enormous,
   your handmade sky-jewelry,

Moon and stars mounted in their settings.
   Then I look at my micro-self and wonder,

> Why do you bother with us?
> Why take a second look our way?
> (Ps. 8:3–4 THE MESSAGE)

Bruce Waltke notes, "His creation reveals his immeasurable power, his bewildering imagination and wisdom, and his immortality and transcendence."[2] It also reveals the spirit of generosity accompanying his presence and every activity in which he's engaged. Where there's smoke, there's fire. And where God is (everywhere), a halo of abundant giving radiates.

It's difficult to quantify a virtue with a formula, like: $F = m*a$ (force equals mass times acceleration). But we might say generosity is at its essence a measurement of abundance. Generosity equals a spirit of unselfishness multiplied by quantity: $G = u*q$. It's giving anything—talent, time, treasure (and more)—freely, abundantly, wholeheartedly, happily, for the good and well-being of another. You know it when you see it.

The Israelites saw it, up close and personal. And it went beyond manna from heaven and footwear that lasted forty years.

First, they observed God generously employ his power to rescue them after four centuries of bondage. He recruited a reluctant shepherd named Moses to represent his people and act as their military general. After several appearances before Pharaoh, a series of unpleasant-to-deadly plagues, and a final warning to their captor-in-chief, Moses secured permission to escort the Hebrews out of Egypt.

God made sure they didn't walk away empty-handed. He somehow inspired the Egyptians to be favorably disposed toward this people of his, so when the Hebrews asked for parting gifts—silver, gold, and clothing—the Egyptians complied. Storybook ending, right? Not so fast. Soon after their victorious march out of captivity, the plot twisted like a salty pretzel. Pharaoh flinched. He floundered. He flip-flopped. Couldn't stand the thought of a liberated labor force. He mustered his army, issued orders, and chased down his slaves like his kingdom depended on it.

> The Egyptians—all Pharaoh's horses and chariots, horsemen and troops—pursued the Israelites and overtook them as they camped by the sea. . . . As Pharaoh approached, the Israelites looked up, and there were the Egyptians, marching after them. They were terrified and cried out to the Lord.
>
> (Ex. 14:9-10)

This wasn't part of the script, was it? You might say the Israelites were pardoned by the president, on their way home from prison, and planning a priceless future. Then a firing squad pulls them over?

Trapped between the devil and the deep Red Sea, desperation overwhelms the Israelites. With disaster imminent, the walls close in. Roadblock ahead, burnt bridge behind. Nowhere to run, nowhere to hide. What just happened? With their collective flight-or-fight mechanism activated, the Israelites freeze and cry out to the Lord.

Ever been there, standing in similar sandals? Out of hope at the end of your rope? Crying for help because you're helpless on your own?

Maybe you weren't physically imprisoned, and your issue wasn't life or death—but it felt that way. Or maybe it feels that way today because your problems aren't behind you. Maybe you're stuck now, with your . . .

finances lean.

job in jeopardy.

marriage shaky.

family fighting.

diagnosis frightening.

friends few and far between.

You're facing a giant, feeling alone, hanging on for dear life.

Whatever the case, take heart. The Great Giver, your Rescuer and Redeemer, is strong.

With the Israelites wallowing in fear, babbling nonsense, Moses speaks: "Do not be afraid. Stand firm and you will see the deliverance the Lord will bring you today" (Ex. 14:13). What happens next? The Lord parts water. The Israelites are emancipated on a dry highway. The sea swallows the Egyptian army and they're never seen again.

Prophets and priests, kings and commoners would talk about this event for centuries to come. It's a picture of God's power—illustrating grace and goodness—*generously* applied.

But wait, there's more.

During this exodus, God was generous with his presence, too. Fully engaged in their plight, he was with them, guiding every step like a boy scout leading a blind person across a busy city street. In a pillar of cloud by day (offering shade from the sun) and fire by night (lighting the dark) God led them and never left them.

That's so like God. Our Father wants to be with us. It makes him happy.

After Moses died, God appointed Joshua to escort the Israelites over the finish line and into the Promised Land. How did God inspire the young warrior to lead on, stay strong, be courageous? Simple. God told Joshua he'd be with him. "I will never leave you nor forsake you" (Josh. 1:5). "The Lord your God will be with you wherever you go" (v. 9). What a gift.

It's the same gift Jesus offers us. After handing out marching orders in the Great Commission—go make disciples—our Savior says, "And surely I am with you always, to the very end of the age" (Matt. 28:20). That's a long time. He didn't say:

I'll be with you until the end of the month, or at least next Tuesday.

I'll be with you until my schedule clutters up.

I'll be with you until you get over the hump.

I'll be with you if you stay on my good side.

I'll be with you if you show up at church every week.

I'll be with you if you tithe.

I'll be with you if you promise to be perfect, like me.

No, there's no "with you, if you" language from Jesus. He's with you for the long haul. Jesus was with you yesterday, he's with you today, and he'll be with you tomorrow. You might say Jesus is generous with his time. And he wants to spend it with people like you.

If you're in doubt, ask Zacchaeus, the crooked tax collector.

Ask Lazarus, the friend he wept for.

Ask the bungling fishermen, his budding entourage.

Ask blind Bartimaeus or curious Nicodemus.

Ask Jairus' daughter or Peter's mother-in-law.

Ask the centurion or the woman at the well who had five husbands.

Ask the children he laughed with, the lepers he healed, the thousands he fed.

Ask the little, the least, the lost, and the lonely. The "bedraggled, beat-up, burnt-out, and burdened."[3] Go ahead, ask a partridge in a pear tree for heaven's sake. You might even ask my friend Judy Reid. But you'll have to wait until you get to heaven.

Judy Reid had cancer. She was single, alone, and too young to die. I was a nervous twenty-something-year-old when I ventured into Moffit Cancer Center for a pastoral visit, highlighted Bible in hand. I had no clue how to comfort my bedridden friend, but thankfully, words came easy. I'll never forget our half-hour together. *She* comforted *me*. My tears that day flowed not from sadness but amazement as she spoke of her Savior and the peace she felt about whatever came next. Judy knew Jesus was with her—actually *with* her—and that was enough. His presence, as real as the furniture in the room, was oxygen for her soul. Of course, we prayed for a miraculous healing, but she had already surrendered the outcome. I learned more about faith that day from Judy than from any sermon or seminary lecture I'd ever heard.

Jesus had time for Judy. He has time for you, too. He's generous with his presence.

If you're still skeptical about the nearness of Jesus, perhaps it's an awareness problem. Consider the last time you thought you were alone but weren't. Someone snuck up behind you. You walked around a blind corner and nearly bumped into an oncoming stranger. You got so lost in thought you forgot you had company. Whatever. The point is you were startled when you suddenly realized the presence of another person right there with you.

That's exactly what happened to Jacob.

It had been a long day. Jacob settled down for the evening. He laid his head on a stone, slipped into a deep sleep, and dreamed. He envisioned a stairway to heaven with angels ascending and descending its steps. Above the stairway towered God, who announced his identity, delivered a message of promise and blessing, and assured Jacob, "I am with you and will watch over you wherever you go" (Gen. 28:15). "When Jacob awoke from his sleep he thought, 'Surely the Lord is in this place and I was not aware of it'" (v. 16). Ah! A sacred moment indeed. Jacob embraced the Lord as his God, set up a memorial stone to mark the event, and promised to give God a tenth of whatever God gave him.

Perhaps it's time for you to awaken and realize God is in this place, wherever this place is. He is so generous with his presence that (like it or not) you can't escape it.

Question: "Lord, where can I go and flee your presence?"
Answer: "Nowhere."

Is there anyplace I can go to avoid your Spirit?
to be out of your sight?

If I climb to the sky, you're there!
If I go underground, you're there!

If I flew on morning's wings
   to the far western horizon,

You'd find me in a minute—
   you're already there waiting!

   (Ps. 139:7-10 THE MESSAGE)

From God's presence you can neither run nor hide. Come to cognitive rest on this reality: You have his full attention. He's not bored with you. He doesn't have better things to do. He is with you because he loves—and even *likes*—you. Yes, you.

Let's circle back to the Israelites on their desert journey. It lasts awhile, say, forty years. Already generous with his power and presence, God also displays openhandedness by providing for their physical needs. Shoes never wear out. Clothes last for decades. Bread comes from heaven, water from a rock. Whatever they require, perfectly timed. When they tire of manna and beg for meat, God gives them quail. He piles it three feet deep, miles wide. Be careful what you ask for. When God gives, he's not stingy.

God didn't ignore a single need. He gave the Israelites commandments to guide them and people to lead them. He gave them victory in battles and a Promised Land. He gave them milk and honey and hope and a future. He gave them captivating stories to tell their children. Whatever they needed, God provided.

Imagine a curious child inquiring about God's unstoppable, incomparable generosity. Can you hear a small voice asking, "Why, Mommy? Do you know, Daddy? Why does he do it? Why does God give so much?"

Your face brightens. You know the answer.

"God is *love*, dear child. And love *gives*."

For God so loved the world he *gave*.

In early March 2022, a team of scientists and researchers located the remains of *Endurance*, the ship used by Ernest Shackleton in his Imperial Trans-Antarctic Expedition. Nearly two miles deep, the 144-foot wooden vessel slept on the icy floor of the Weddell Sea for 106 years. If you read accounts of this survival story, you'll realize the ship did not go down easy.

Endurance was a strong vessel, her sides nearly two feet thick in most places. For five months she faithfully carried the twenty-eight men onboard toward their destination, but merely a day or so before expected landfall, the voyage halted when ice locked the ship in a frozen prison. Immobilized, creaking, groaning, she lasted nine painful months. On November 21, 1915, millions of tons of ice won the standoff, crushing *Endurance* and spitting her to the bottom of the sea.

Now what? Shackleton and his crew salvaged three lifeboats and a host of supplies. They set up camp on a giant ice floe. But imagine their unfathomable challenges: ferocious weather, fickle ocean currents, uncertain food supplies, unspoken fears, hundreds of miles from civilization, and no *Endurance* to bring them home. This was the most inhospitable place on Earth. They might as well have been on the dark side of the moon.

One fact they knew for sure: they were completely on their own. No rescue team would save them. The Coast Guard wasn't coming.

What follows is an astonishing tale of perseverance, bravery, leadership, cooperation, and sheer willpower. The astounding outcome: all twenty-eight men lived and made it back to where their expedition began two years earlier. In all of history, few survival stories compare.

Shackleton did something physically that cannot be done spiritually. You cannot save yourself. With or without endurance, no amount of perseverance, skill, luck, or desire can save you. Only Jesus can save you.

King Jesus to the rescue.

When you were shipwrecked, marooned on a giant block of floating ice, tossed by winds and waves, distant from the priceless life you were born to live—cold, wet, hungry, hopeless, and helpless—Jesus came to save you. You didn't find him. He found you. And he gave his life for you.

"For God so loved the world that he gave his one and only Son, that whoever believes in him shall not perish but have eternal life" (John 3:16). Believe it or not, this unthinkable act of charity brought Jesus pleasure. "For the joy set before him he endured the cross . . ." (Heb. 12:2).

How priceless! What a mighty, happy, generous God we serve.

CHAPTER TWO

• • •

BORN FOR THIS

*The most important days in your life are
the day you are born and the day you find out why.*

MARK TWAIN

our birth certificate provides proof of your existence. In Florida, the two-page document from the Office of Vital Statistics contains fifty-seven blank fields to populate. Child's Name (first, middle, last, suffix). Sex. Date of Birth (that seems kind of important). Birth weight. Time of Birth. County of Birth. Place where birth occurred (hospital, home, doctor's office, etc.). City, Town, or Location of Birth. Lots of data about your grand entrance into this world.

Then there's information about your mother and father. Their birthdates and their parents' birthdates. Addresses, education, race, signatures, and so on. Of course, there's an entire section for administrative purposes, including medical and health questions. Your birth certificate contains every pertinent detail about your earthly arrival except one: *why you were born*. There is no fifty-eighth field marked "Purpose."

Who are you? Where did you come from? Where are you going? And what are you here to do? These are lofty questions. Questions you might have pondered. Questions a wise, wealthy man set out to answer 3,000 years ago. The search for meaning and happiness is not a new endeavor. Who wants to live like a modern-day Sisyphus, the ancient Greek figure sentenced to eternal absurdity, rolling a boulder up a steep hill only to watch it tumble back down every time he reached the summit?

The Old Testament book Ecclesiastes chronicles an exhaustive exploration of life's purpose. It ends with a concise declaration: "Fear God and keep his commandments, for this is the whole duty of all mankind" (Eccles. 12:13 ESV). The inspired sage who authored this narrative (we'll call him the Teacher)[1] didn't jump to conclusions or take anyone's word for it. He made it his personal quest to study and explore all life had to offer, hoping to discover something—anything—that wasn't meaningless, "a chasing after the wind" (Eccles. 1:14).

Can you relate? Have you ever thought: "What's the point?" I hope so. "If we neglect to ponder the questions that emerge from our depths, we will continue to operate autonomously, and we will live an unconscious, unreflective, accidental life."[2]

The Teacher's mission is urgent. He understands the brevity of life. Generations come and go; here today, gone tomorrow. "You are a mist that appears for a little while and then vanishes" (James 4:14). Although your birth and death certificates might cite dates spanning eighty-plus years, as you age those years zoom by faster and scrunch closer together. The clock ticks. The calendar turns. Seasons come. Seasons go. You thought you had more time.

In John Lennon's final interview on December 5, 1980, the former Beatle talked about touring again. He said, "We just might do it . . . there's plenty of time, right? Plenty of time." Three days later, at forty years old, John Lennon drew his final breath.

While the sun rises and the sun sets, while winds blow and streams flow (Eccles. 1:5-7), how will you find purpose and meaning? From the world? Social media? Wall Street? Main Street? The latest, most popular, going-viral, celebrity influencer? Be careful. The Apostle Paul warns, "Do not conform to the pattern of this world, but be transformed by the renewing of your mind" (Rom. 12:2). John agrees, "Do not love the world or the things in the world. . . . For all that is in the world—the desires of the flesh and the desires of the eyes and pride of life—is not from the Father but is from the world" (1 John 2:15-16 ESV).

The Teacher's firsthand experience with worldly exploits left him hollow and unsatisfied. He sought wisdom, knowledge, understanding. *Meaningless*. He indulged in pleasure and laughter, washing it down with a chalice of wine. *Meaningless*. He undertook grand projects: houses, vineyards, gardens, orchards, and parks. *Meaningless*. He amassed possessions: slaves, herds, flocks, silver, gold, and a harem of delightful women. Alas, even this was meaningless, chasing after the wind. The Teacher hated everything he worked for, knowing he'd have to leave it all behind to someone who didn't toil for it (Eccles. 2:21).

We nod in agreement grasping the futility of it all, convinced we're savvy enough to avoid trivial pursuits. We won't be duped. And yet, there is always . . .

One more ladder to climb.

One more goal to reach.

One more project to finish.

One more promotion to earn.

One more challenge to conquer, place to visit, mountain to scale.

One more degree to frame, dollar to save, item to own, award to earn.

One more race to win, title to hold, trophy to hoist, and party to throw.

Just one more. One more thing to check off our bucket list. As Rich Mullins sang, "Everybody I know says they need just one thing, and what they really mean is they need just one thing *more*."[3]

When will we learn? Guzzling an ocean of salt water won't quench our thirst.

In the end, acknowledging both his fruitless attempt to master the future and the vacuous nature of human striving, the Teacher surrendered.[4] He turned to God as the source of meaning. His new pursuit: honor God's commandments and enjoy his gifts on a daily basis. One theologian writes:

> The preacher (teacher) wishes to deliver us from a
> rosy-colored, self-confident, godless life, with its
> inevitable cynicism and bitterness, and from
> trusting in wisdom, pleasure, wealth, and human
> justice or integrity. He wishes to drive us to see
> that God is there, that he is good and generous,
> and that only such an outlook makes life coherent
> and fulfilling.[5]

One day, out of curiosity, I googled "What is the meaning of life?" I could have clicked over one billion links for more information. I didn't have that much time. I'm sticking with the foregone conclusion: *Fear God and keep his commandments.* Certainly, we must parse this broad declaration to find practical daily life rhythms, but the Teacher's wisdom gets us out of the starting blocks. Let's keep going.

Completed in 1647, The Westminster Shorter Catechism answers 107 doctrinal questions that distill and illuminate biblical truth. The opening question-and-answer probes deeply: "What is the chief end of man? *Man's chief end is to glorify God and enjoy him forever.*" Fully unpacking this instructive statement exceeds the scope of this chapter but open the suitcase and here's what you see: Live a God-centered rather than self-centered life.[6]

Return to the garden where the human race was planted. Sneak a glimpse of God's original blueprint. Our true identity—who we are—is rooted in the incomprehensible reality that God took dust and formed us in his image, a claim no other object or life form can make. So yes, you're special. You were created to represent and reflect the King of the kingdom. His life and presence dwell in you. If you accept the premise that God is the Great Giver and you're crafted in his image, you'll realize generosity resides in your DNA. That's right, you're genetically wired to give. Frogs jump, birds fly, horses run, mosquitos bite. Humans? Well, humans *give.* At least, that's how we're designed.

When we let our light shine before others, they'll see our good deeds and glorify our Father in heaven.[7] Expressing your embedded generosity in Spirit-led ways glorifies God, of course, but it also releases balloons of joy in a broken world. And when colorful balloons rise in the sky people look up. And smile.

Generosity will always be an integral part of glorifying God and enjoying him forever. You were blessed to be a blessing. It's what you're here to do. And the quality of your life depends on it.

When Paul instructed Timothy to "command those who are rich in this present world" (a description of many people reading this book) "to do good, to be rich in good deeds, and to be generous and willing to share," he affirmed *we'd* be the big winners, rewarded with "life that is truly life" (1 Tim. 6:17-19). No more chasing the wind. No more meaninglessness. Your calling and purpose—to bless others generously—is wrapped in your identity as a child of God.

A brief passage in the New Testament punctuates the emphasis on heartfelt, happiness-generating generosity. The story involves Jesus, some Pharisees, and a legal exam.

Jesus regularly astonished crowds with relatable stories and revealing teaching. It's no surprise people approached him with pressing questions. (Don't you have a question you'd love to ask him today?) One illuminating day a group of Pharisees seized an opportunity to query Jesus. After they noticed their rivals, the Sadducees, silenced by Jesus' response to a convoluted scenario about marriage and the resurrection, they huddled up. It wasn't unusual for religious leaders to debate matters of the law. The Pharisees identified 613 specific commandments and their order of importance mattered. So, these Pharisees nominated one of their legal experts to pose a stumper to Jesus: "Teacher, which is the greatest commandment in the Law?" (Matt. 22:36). Perhaps they placed bets on how Jesus would respond.

BORN FOR THIS | 33

He'll quote our prophet Micah, "And what does the Lord require of you? To act justly and to love mercy, and to walk humbly with your God" (Mic. 6:8).

No, it'll be one of the Big Ten etched on the tablets Moses lugged down the mountain.

He won't know the answer. We can't even agree, and nobody studies the law more than us.

The words Jesus spoke next were not unfamiliar to his listeners. "Love the Lord your God with all your heart and with all your soul and with all your mind. This is the first and greatest commandment" (Matt. 22:37-38). But Jesus goes for extra credit. He gives them the second greatest commandment, too: "Love your neighbor as yourself" (v. 39). Then he drives home the significance of these words, excerpted from Deuteronomy and Leviticus, by saying, "All the law and the prophets hang on these two commandments" (v. 40).

Really? Everything? C'mon. Our entire list of do's and don'ts? This, that, and the other thing? The complete catalog of right and wrong?

Yes, everything.

Everything snuggles under the blanket of these two congruent commandments. From circumcision to tithing. From honoring the Sabbath to practicing sorcery. From taking revenge to praying for your persecutors. You name it and this duo of decrees covers it: trusting, forgiving, praising, sharing, celebrating, confessing, honoring, resting, stealing, hating, gossiping, profaning, coveting, testing, bearing a grudge, oppressing the weak ... we could go on all day.

Love God and love people. The answer to the final exam. Easy to say, hard to master.

But it's what you're here to do.

You were born to love.

And remember, love *gives*.

The first words in Shel Silverstein's classic children's book, *The Giving Tree*, set the stage for the tender tale: "Once there was a tree... and she loved a little boy."[8] If you overlook that sentence, you miss the underlying reason for all the giving that follows.

Initially, the tree's gifts are playful and modest. A trunk to climb, branches to swing on, shade to rest under, apples to eat. But as the boy grows older the gifts get costlier. When the boy asks the tree for a house, she gives all her branches for construction material. We know this act of generosity pleases the tree, because after each episode of gift-giving, the author sneaks in a revealing refrain: "And the tree was happy."

Years pass and the aged boy returns to the tree, now requesting a boat. The tree complies again, sacrificing her entire trunk. Assuming she has nothing left to give and knowing the boy is sailing away, the tree isn't so happy anymore. But the story isn't finished.

After a lengthy absence, the weary boy returns to his beloved friend for the last time. His tired eyes fall on the tree. Wrinkles etch his sagging face. Bones ache, hands tremble. The elderly boy's shuffling steps are so slow he'd lose a race with a three-legged turtle. All he wants is peace and quiet and somewhere to rest. Is that too much to ask? The tree, now nothing but a stump, offers the boy the only thing she has left to give: a place to sit. The boy bends his creaky knees and settles down. Ahh!

And the tree was happy.

The giving tree knew why she was planted on this earth. So did Jesus.

On his last full day on this planet, while eating the Passover meal with his inner circle of friends, Jesus knew the time had come for him to leave this world. How would he spend his final hours? How will you spend yours?

Maybe you'll recount your accomplishments. Watch a mental video of favorite memories. Flip through an album of treasured pictures. Wax nostalgic with family and friends. Embrace your dearest loved ones. Give thanks for the priceless life you've been privileged to live. Pray to God like never before. As a confident believer, why not pop the cork on a bottle of champagne as you look forward to homecoming with the Lord? You might do any number of things as the sand in your hourglass drains its last grains.

Jesus had options, too.

HE COULD HAVE DECIDED TO STAY. Put off the inevitable. At only thirty-three earth-years old, why not spend more time wearing flesh? Hanging around his handiwork—he created all things—sounds way better than hanging on a cross. Weren't there more flowers to smell and seas to sail? More needy to feed and lepers to cure? Surely, there were more places to go, people to meet, and things to do.

HE COULD HAVE DELIVERED A LECTURE. One final discourse to cram a crucial lesson into his disciples' heads. His apprentices had recently been arguing about their own greatness and needed an old-fashioned, finger-wagging, talking-to. How about one more parable to set them straight?

HE COULD HAVE DEMANDED A TRIBUTE. Why not throw a going away party fit for a king? Roll out the red carpet. Set out the fine dishes. Make wine out of water. Hire the premier caterer in Jerusalem. For entertainment, they could watch highlight reels of Jesus all night. The Miracle Worker himself could narrate.

There's me healing a man born blind. I did that with mud made from my spit. How cool is that?

Hey, there's me doing the moonwalk on the Sea of Galilee. Not so easy is it, Peter?

You guys remember this fishing trip, don't you? Aren't you glad you listened to me? "Put the nets down here," I said.

Oh, you gotta watch this, there's me calling Lazarus out of his tomb. Hear my deep voice? I sound like a radio announcer. "Lazarus, come forth." He was dead for four days, you know. Watch when he first walks out . . . he looks like a mummy.

HE COULD HAVE DEVELOPED A STRATEGY. He knew he had come from God and was returning to God. Why not create a tactical plan to spread the gospel? All the X's and O's, not just the announcement we read in Acts 1:8: "You will be my witnesses in Jerusalem, and in all Judea and Samaria, and to the ends of the earth." What kind of plan is that? Let's do case studies, hire consultants, conduct research. We can focus on core competencies, operate with economies of scale, and capitalize on horizontal integration. Who's creating the marketing campaign?

HE COULD HAVE DECIPHERED A MYSTERY. In spite of

spending so much time with Jesus, the apostles often appeared clueless. Truth is, they deserve some slack. God is more complicated than a game of tic-tac-toe. Too bad Jesus didn't pull back the curtain and reveal some answers to profound mysteries.

I've got an easy way to understand the trinity . . .

Oh, you want to know why evil exists? Here's the answer . . .

Let me tell you exactly why you're experiencing all that pain and suffering . . .

The reason I created rats, bats, roaches, rattlesnakes, and eight-legged hairy spiders, is . . .

HE COULD HAVE DESTROYED JUDAS. Jesus pointed out his betrayer. Most would have wanted revenge—more than just a verbal assault.

So here we are on that fateful evening 2,000 years ago. The night before he died. What *did* Jesus do?

> He got up from the meal, took off his outer
> clothing, and wrapped a towel around his waist.
> After that, he poured water into a basin and began
> to wash his disciples' feet, drying them with the
> towel that was wrapped around him.
>
> (John 13:4-5)

Highly unexpected. Deeply revealing. The demeaning task was fit for a slave, not a king. And yet, Jesus washed and dried twenty-four feet that night. Two belonged to Judas the betrayer. And two belonged to Peter the denier. Although Peter resisted, Jesus persisted, "Unless I wash you, you have no part with me" (John 13:8).

After the foot cleaning, Jesus took a seat and tossed out a question, "Do you understand what I have done for you?" He did not wait for an answer.

> I have set you an example that you should do as I have done for you. Very truly I tell you, no servant is greater than his master, nor is a messenger greater than the one who sent him. Now that you know these things, you will be blessed if you do them.
>
> (John 13:15-17)

On his final night, Jesus displays his true colors. It was not time to extend his stay, deliver a lecture, demand a tribute, develop a strategy, decipher a mystery, or destroy an enemy. It was time to serve. Aren't you glad Jesus explained why he washed sticky dirt off smelly feet? And be honest, does his closing statement—perform a sacrificial act of service and you'll be happy—surprise you?

You will be blessed? Really?

Yes. Because you were born to live a priceless life.

CHAPTER THREE

• • •

WHAT HOLDS
YOU BACK?

For I have the desire to do what is right,
but not the ability to carry it out.

THE APOSTLE PAUL

*T*he first time I tried to fly, something went terribly wrong. I was a little past kindergarten age and slightly more adventurous than I am today. One summer morning, while neighborhood kids loitered near our house, we kicked cans and brainstormed how to spend the day. My older sister Cathi came up with a brilliant idea. A crazy idea. An idea that seized our attention. She convinced me if I jumped off the roof holding an open umbrella over my head, I could fly like Mary Poppins. Amazing!

At first, I was skeptical. But Cathi assured me she'd tried it herself and it really worked: "You just kind of float in the air." I had long dreamed of flying like Mary Poppins. The neighborhood gang goaded me on with reckless enthusiasm. No one had any better ideas. So, of course, I had to give it a shot.

Cathi leaned Daddy's ladder against a rickety backyard gutter. My rag-tag audience circled. I crept up the wooden rungs, one slow-motion step at a time. My hands trembled. My head fogged. My heart giddy-upped faster than a Kentucky Derby thoroughbred racing down the homestretch. I sprang open the umbrella and began to navigate off the top rung of the ladder onto the roof, where I'd stage my launch and soar like Mary Poppins. And that's the last thing I remember.

They said when I hit the ground, I was out for a good, long time. I woke up on our front porch, in Mommy's arms, as the wail of ambulance sirens pierced the air. I survived my crash landing—little boys bounce like rubber—and learned a couple of important lessons that day.

1. Never trust your sister.

2. Flying like Mary Poppins is more complicated than it looks.

Sometimes generosity is complicated, too. Invitations to give come your way and you want to be generous but not crazy. You're willing to sacrifice but not suffer. You listen to the Spirit but your flesh whispers, too: *Let's not go overboard.*

What will you do? How do you decide? What's holding you back?

In their book, *Passing the Plate: Why American Christians Don't Give Away More Money*, authors Christian Smith and Michael O. Emerson seek to piece together the puzzling reasons why, despite significant stores of wealth, "most American Christians are remarkably ungenerous."[1] Only thirteen percent of evangelicals tithe—the practice of giving ten percent of one's income to the church.[2] Historically, followers of Jesus give in a range averaging two to three percent of what they earn. But most drearily, "half of all evangelical Protestants contribute less than one percent of their total income to church *and* charity."[3] Believe it or not, many give absolutely nothing. Zero. Zilch. Nada. Not a dirty dime.

Admittedly, these gloomy facts don't tell the whole story. Who knows, perhaps people who aren't giving money are generous in other ways. Regardless, something is still very wrong with this picture.

We owe every breath to the Great Giver. Generosity resides in our DNA. We're instructed to honor the Lord with our wealth, the first and best of our earnings.[4] When it comes to money and possessions, we're warned, encouraged, commanded, and taught to prioritize a generous lifestyle that considers the needs of others and bears witness to our faith. We're told to give—with good measure, pressed down, shaken together, running over—and we'll be given back with the same measure.[5] And true to God's word, "generous people tend to receive back goods that are even more valuable than those they gave: happiness, health, a sense of purpose in life, and personal growth."[6] In spite of all this, too often we stumble in the area of generosity. Why is this so? How can this be?

Before we tackle the question, take a fresh breath. And another. If you feel a cloud of guilt, pride, or ambivalence settling in, clear the air. You're reading this book to move forward in your generosity journey, not sink into emotional quicksand. Self-deprecating feelings won't help. Allow them to serve as a wakeup call, but don't permit them to linger.

Guilt is a thief, a barrier, a block wall that separates you from happiness and cages you in the prison of past actions.

Pride is the "utmost evil, the complete anti-God state of mind," according to C. S. Lewis, and not a welcome passenger on this journey.

Ambivalence is a ho-hum, this-isn't-such-a-big-deal philosophy and may mean you've already called it quits or are simply overwhelmed by it all.

Accept the reality that emotional tension exists—like an uninvited trespasser difficult to evict. This tension camps in our heads, suppressing the generous tendencies our souls desire to nourish. Most people admit they *should* give more and indeed *desire* to give more.[7] But how much will you release to others and how much will you keep for yourself? Do competing impulses confuse and stifle you? Join the club.

The apostle Paul empathizes, confessing, "For I do not understand my own actions. For I do not do what I want, but I do the very thing I hate" (Rom. 7:15 ESV). "For I have the desire to do what is right, but not the ability to carry it out" (v. 18 ESV). Giving lavishly, like jumping off the roof with a magical umbrella, is both exhilarating and frightening. Sometimes it's hard to take the leap. And we frequently make excuses to justify our reluctance.

Raising our kids, we had a zero-tolerance policy on name calling. Of course, with four children, occasional quarrels are part of life. Siblings square off on opposite sides. Friction fills the air. Years ago, our sweet little Melissa, who was four or five years old at the time, got so frustrated with her older sister she couldn't contain it any longer. She cleverly found a loophole around our policy and shouted, "Melanie, if I COULD call you a pig, I WOULD call you a pig... but I'm not allowed!"

Are you tempted to think, *If I COULD give more, I WOULD give more? But...*

I'm on a fixed income.

I'm swimming in debt.

These kids are expensive.

We're saving for college.

Inflation is killing us.

We don't have health insurance.

There's no egg in my retirement nest.

If I could give more, I would give more.

What's your loophole?

Perhaps you shift focus onto the potential beneficiaries of your generosity. You tell yourself, *They don't need it. Don't deserve it. Won't appreciate it. They'll squander it. I've already given enough. It won't make much of a difference. They won't properly thank me.* (If God ever feels this way when he gives to us, it certainly hasn't deterred him. Thank God!) While it is wise to evaluate how a charitable organization (or individual) might steward your gift, if you can't find *anything* or *anyone* worthy of your generosity, the problem might be you.

Of all the reasons that hold us back, one eclipses all others: a *scarcity mentality.* We don't have enough, or so we think. This mindset differs from greed—an insatiable quest for more (we'll cover that later). A scarcity mentality feels ominous, like being lost in a desert with food supplies shrinking and canteens running dry. Our lives lack something vital—money, time, energy, whatever—and prospects to resolve our deficiency are slim. Like a game of musical chairs, there are not enough seats to go around.[8]

Scarcity scares us. And living in a prolonged state of scarcity *scars* us. The trauma convinces us to preserve our limited assets. You must protect your future, right? How can you give away something you don't have enough of?

That's what a poor widow wonders when Elijah asks her for a slice of bread. By way of divine judgment, it hadn't rained in years. No dew on the grass either. When the drought begins, the Lord sends the prophet to a hideout east of Jordan and tells him, "You will drink from the brook, and I have directed the ravens to supply you with food there" (1 Kings 17:4). Meals-on-wings is an unusual delivery system and we're not told where the ravens acquired the food, but these ancient living drones came through, flying in fresh bread and meat for breakfast and dinner. (Maybe lunch was leftovers?)

The brook dries up and it's time for Elijah to move on. "Go at once to Zarephath," said the Lord, "I have directed a widow there to supply you with food" (v. 9). Would it not make more sense for God to use a wealthy land baron or bank president or grocery store owner to provide meals for the prophet? Nevertheless, even a starving widow seems like an upgrade from a flock of ravens.

Elijah finds the widow gathering sticks at the town gate. His parched lips long for moisture. "Would you bring me a little water in a jar?" he asks (v. 10). The widow complies, but as she sets off to fulfill the order, Elijah calls out a second request. "And bring me, please, a piece of bread" (v. 11). It's interesting he says "please." Because this is an "Are-you-serious?" moment. Bread? Really? At a time like this, in the midst of a famine?

"I have nothing baked," she replies, "only a handful of flour in a jar and a little olive oil in a jug" (v. 12). She informs Elijah her intentions were to go home, make a final meal for her and her son, then die. There's not enough bread to share. Sorry, Elijah.

The prophet reassures her, telling the widow to go home and

follow her plan. "But first, make a small loaf of bread for me from what you have and bring it to me..." (v. 13).

Wait, what? But *first*?

Let's pause to review the situation. Elijah makes modest requests: a *little* water and a *small* loaf of bread. The water, sure, but for a widow with only a handful of flour in a jug and a little oil in a jar, giving away even a small loaf of bread meant no food for her and her son.

"But *first*," says Elijah. *First*, make some bread, bring it to me, and *then* make something for yourself and your son. The widow must suspect Elijah has a hearing problem. Or no idea how to bake bread. *If I empty my jug and jar for you, what's left for my boy and me? Is one last meal before we die too much to ask?*

Back to the story. Elijah continues, "For this is what the Lord, the God of Israel, says: 'The jar of flour will not be used up and the jug of oil will not run dry until the day the Lord sends rain on the land'" (v. 14).

How cool is that? The widow trusts the prophet and follows his instructions. Smart move. True prophets never lie. Her jug and jar didn't see the inside of a dishwasher for a while. As promised, they stayed full until the next downpour drenched the thirsty dirt.

So what's our problem? We have packed pantries—full jugs and overflowing jars—but we behave like we're down to our final meal. A homeless person panhandles for spare change and we have no change to spare. The church takes up an extra offering to help orphans overseas and your thoughts drift to the school supplies your own kids need. Your spouse asks for a single Chick-fil-A waffle fry and you, cheeks bulging with food, inspect the container to see how many are left. You don't want to run out of fries.

As I scanned titles on bookshelves in our local library recently, a man I'd seen near the front desk approached me and humbly asked for fifteen cents. Fifteen cents? What does anyone need fifteen cents for? Turns out, this job-hunter wanted to print one copy of his resume. I never carry coins in my pocket and rarely keep cash in my wallet, but I found two singles tucked behind my credit cards. I passed him a dollar; he promised he'd return with change. "Oh, don't worry about it," I said, waving him off. But he tracked me down a few minutes later. "Thank you!" he said, dropping three quarters and a dime into my hand.

It brings me joy to imagine my fifteen-cent gift helped an industrious man find a decent job. On the flip side, it troubles me to think about all the rewarding—and, of course, much costlier—giving opportunities I've passed over in my life. What about you? Do you have any regrets?

Oskar Schindler did. He generously used his financial resources to help an estimated 1,200 Jews escape Nazi death camps during World War II, but a closing scene in the film *Schindler's List* depicts the man agonizing over what else he might have done. "I could have got more out," he cries, "I could have got more." "I threw away so much money." Schindler points to his car and says, "Ten more people." A gold pin, he claims, was worth two more people.[9] His comments are reminiscent of A. W. Tozer's insight, "By the judgment seat of Christ, my service will not be judged by how much I've done, but by how much I could have done."

How much can we do?

Not much, if we're paralyzed by a scarcity mentality.

When the fear of not having enough inhibits our generosity, we hold on, pull back, cling to, and stockpile. *And* we miss the blessing of helping a man find a job or saving a starving soul from certain death. Fortunately, we can overcome this deceptive mindset, but it requires a shift in perspective. It's not an effortless endeavor. But with God, change is possible.

A proper assessment of our personal resources is essential. Time arrives in blocks of twenty-four hours per day, seven blocks per week. Nobody gets more, nobody less. Talent, giftedness, and abilities are uniquely allocated by our Creator and enhanced by training, effort, and education. We all have something to offer. Money and possessions—what we typically refer to as treasure—are unevenly distributed. Here's where we get really messed up. Most of us are wealthier than we know.

Line up 100 random people from every corner of the world in order of their income, highest to lowest. If you earn $30,000 per year, ninety-five people stand behind you.[10] A person with a $100,000 income is first in line. Put another way, imagine you're one of 296 passengers flying Delta, boarding a Boeing 777 to New York (or anywhere).[11] The highest earners get the best seats. A $20,000 annual income scores you a spot in first class. Where are you sitting? Are you enjoying the extra space and free drinks?

Now calculate your net worth by adding up your cash, home equity, stocks, bonds, real estate, automobiles, jewelry—every item you own—then deduct your liabilities. If the number totals more than $10,000, you're wealthier than over half the people on the planet.[12] Does your net worth exceed $100,000? If so, eighty-eight percent of the human population has less than you. Inevitably, these exact statistics oscillate over time, but entrenched global financial disparity remains. (Even when accounting for the varying cost of goods sold in different cities, regions, and countries, of course.) Perhaps this knowledge can sober minds accustomed to incessant upward comparisons. Look in the downward direction and you'll see 811 million people going to bed hungry tonight.[13]

Regardless of where you rank on the income and wealth scale, you wouldn't refuse a raise or shred a winning lottery ticket. Because more money means greater financial security, right? Isn't that the cure for a scarcity mentality? Maybe not.

A fascinating study done by Boston College surveyed a sample of the ultra-wealthy. The 165 respondents had an average net worth of $78 million. One-hundred-twenty households enjoyed net assets above $25 million. As a group, they weren't as happy as you might think. Obviously, cash can't solve every problem life flings at you, but you'd imagine these folks would feel well-prepared in the money department. Surprisingly, most of them still experienced thoughts of financial insecurity. Which is like Miss Universe thinking she's ugly. Or Tom Brady in his prime feeling as capable as a third-string, rookie quarterback with a broken right arm. These super-rich folks revealed in order to feel secure they'd need about twenty-five percent more than they currently possessed![14] It's always just a little bit more, isn't it?

Full immunity from the "I-don't-have-enough" disease does not come from shelves lined with full jugs, overflowing jars, or a $25 million net worth. It comes from taking God at his word. Every dollar bill announces, "In God We Trust," a convenient reminder not to put your hope in a piece of paper produced at the U.S. Bureau of Engraving and Printing. Instead, have confidence in God's promises. He's not yet broken one.

"Not one of all the Lord's good promises to Israel failed; every one was fulfilled" (Josh. 21:45).

"The Lord is trustworthy in all he promises and faithful in all he does" (Ps. 145:13).

"For no matter how many promises God has made, they are "Yes" in Christ." (2 Cor. 1:20).

Trusting God is the secret to a life without lack.[15]

But . . . how has he promised to care for your needs?

Will you truly always have enough?

Fair questions. Let's explore them next. The answers are priceless.

CHAPTER FOUR

◆ ◆ ◆

A MATTER OF TRUST

*Trust in the Lord with all your heart
and lean not on your own understanding . . .*

PROVERBS 3:5

*A*re you more valuable than a bird? I hope you answered, "Of course." Now hold that thought.

To the untutored eye, *Young Girl in Profile in Renaissance Dress*, seems like just another artwork of mysterious origin. A pleasant portrait, yes, but nothing extraordinary. Even an expert New York art dealer who shelled out $22,000 for it in 1998 and sold it a decade later for close to her acquisition cost wouldn't have guessed the ultimate value of the piece.[1]

But the artwork's new owner, Peter Silverman, saw something in the chalk and ink drawing others had missed. He suspected the hands that originally brushed the image on vellum belonged to a person with refined talent, so he recruited experts, including art historian Martin Kemp, to investigate. Mr. Kemp worked like a sleuth consumed by an unsolvable mystery. He used sophisticated technology. He analyzed pigments and parchment. He spent a year probing every detail and dimension of the drawing. And his painstaking research paid off. Multispectral digital analysis revealed a smudge on the upper left-hand corner of the canvas, and this smudge, opined Mr. Kemp, was a fingerprint from the hand of a man who lived hundreds of years ago.[2] You might've heard of him: Leonardo da Vinci.

The artwork's value skyrocketed to $160 million.[3] Nothing about the drawing changed, except the knowledge that a Renaissance genius crafted the image. We should note that while some art scholars agreed with Kemp's conclusion, others remain unconvinced. But the point is not lost: A work of art's worth is linked to the identity of its creator.

Your own intrinsic value depends on whose fingerprints smudge your soul. Are you a product of a billions-of-years process of fortuitous evolution? Or do you believe God's pencil sketched your frame on the canvas of your mother's womb? The Bible says you're purposely, fearfully, and wonderfully made.[4] Not a random act of nature but a supernaturally designed masterpiece.

Which brings us back to the bird.

Scripture mentions birds dozens of times. Ravens fed a starving prophet. Pigeons served as sin-offering sacrifices. A dove scouted dry ground after a worldwide flood. Quail sustained Israelites who tired of manna. To Isaiah's listeners, eagles were symbols of power and endurance. Birds served divine purposes as they soared through the Bible and Jesus used them as a trust-teaching tool. "Look at the birds of the air; they do not sow or reap or store away in barns, and yet your heavenly Father feeds them," observed Jesus (Matt. 6:26).

I've noticed the same thing.

On the patch of ten acres where our farmhouse sits, flocks of egrets swarm the sky. Woodpeckers hammer southern pines. Owls coo into the night and roosters welcome the first beams of light. Black crows litter metal rooftops and Red-tailed hawks decorate fence posts like statues—until they come to life and lift off their perches. Lots of avian activity, but never has a bird borrowed my John Deere tractor equipped with the plow attachment. Not once have I witnessed birds plant spring crops or reap a fall harvest. No bird has leased our barn for food storage. The creatures aren't lazy, mind you. They simply rely on God to sustain them.

Jesus points to the birds, then poses the question: "Are you not much more valuable than they?" (Matt. 6:26). Well, of course you are. When God ranks living organisms, you're atmospherically higher on the list than birds.

Jesus doubles down to address another human necessity: clothing.

> See how the flowers of the field grow. They do
> not labor or spin. Yet I tell you that not even
> Solomon in all his splendor was dressed like one
> of these. If that is how God clothes the grass of
> the field, which is here today and tomorrow is
> thrown into the fire, will he not much more
> clothe you—you of little faith?
>
> (Matt. 6:28-30)

You rank higher than flowers, too. All of that to say: Worry not about the basics of life. Jesus knows an anxious heart weighs a person down (Prov. 12:25). And he knows we worry, right?

Are you an anxiety expert? Do you fret about future uncertainties? Do you fear unknown unknowns? Does your imagination wander into swampland where uneasy thoughts evolve from tadpoles into dragons? Do endless cycles of "What If?" scenarios discourage your spirit and taunt your soul? An exhausting existence, for sure.

What if this unexplained pain won't go away?

What if this relationship doesn't work out?

What if I fail at my new job?

What if I make the wrong decision?

What if they think I'm too young?

What if they think I'm too old?

What if my kids (or grandkids) get tangled up with the wrong crowd?

What if they find out who I really, truly am?

What if the money runs out before the end of the month?

We all have a collection of concerns. For many, financial matters rise like cream to the top of the worry list. The truth is, Jesus doesn't want you worrying about money (or anything else).

The God who feeds finches and dresses dandelions knows your needs and won't ignore them. You're too precious to him. "Can a mother forget the infant at her breast, walk away from the baby she bore?" (Isa. 49:15 THE MESSAGE). Don't bet on it. "But even if mothers forget, I'd never forget you—never" (v. 15). After all, your name is tattooed on the palms of God's hands (v. 16). Therefore, follow the Psalmist's habit: "When I am afraid, I put my trust in you" (Ps. 56:3). Then occupy your mind with Jesus' next words, our North Star. "But seek first his kingdom and his righteousness, and all these things will be given to you as well" (Matt. 6:33).

With simple illustrations, the Master reveals where to put your faith and focus.

Trust God.

Seek his kingdom.

God will provide what you require.

Your financial security is not hidden in a bank vault, buried on a tropical island, or waiting at the end of a rainbow's arc. Pursuing riches won't bring peace. Hoarding cash isn't the answer. That's why Jesus' bird and flower comments accompany a warning about wealth accumulation.

> Do not lay up for yourselves treasures on earth,
> where moth and rust destroy, and where thieves
> break in and steal. But lay up for yourselves
> treasures in heaven, where neither moth nor rust
> destroys, and where thieves do not break in and
> steal.
>
> (Matt. 6:19-20 ESV)

I won't forget when the reality of this passage came alive for Mary Ann and me. While we were out one morning, thieves ransacked our home and stole every last piece of valuable jewelry we owned. It wasn't a massive stockpile, but the thoughtful treasures I gave Mary Ann on special occasions over the years carried high sentimental value. Worst of all, we lost family heirlooms dating back over a century, including three generations of wedding rings. Mary Ann asked me not to buy her expensive jewelry again (she prefers horses, actually). In hindsight, we'd both be happier today had we given it all away before crooks had a chance to steal the loot.

Is it wrong to give your beloved partner a sparkly rock or

band of precious metal? (Or a spunky, well-trained quarter horse with decent bloodlines?) Of course not. But it begs the questions:

What do you treasure? And who do you trust?

Trust isn't relying on something already in your pocket. It's believing the train is coming while it's miles down the tracks. It's knowing at midnight that morning draws near. It's a conviction that heaven's treasures last forever, while earth's melt faster than a strawberry popsicle on an August afternoon in Arizona. Faith is being sure of what we hope for and certain of what we don't yet see (Heb. 11:1). And a raindrop of faith is worth more than a river of gold.

Trust acknowledges that the God who made you and loves you will not forsake or abandon you, no matter how hopeless and helpless you feel. Galileo said, "The sun, with all those planets revolving around it and dependent on it, can still ripen a bunch of grapes as if it had nothing else in the universe to do." Likewise, the God who cups the universe in his hands also cares for sparrows and numbers the hairs on your head.

Sometimes it takes a miracle for truth to sink in.

Suppose you come home from work early on Friday. You tell your wife you've invited the entire office over for dinner. Tonight. All 5,000 colleagues and their families. Parking could be a problem. She fakes a "you're-such-a-kidder" laugh and plays along.

"Well, we do have a couple fish in the fridge. I planned to grill them this weekend."

"Yeah," you add, "And I know there's bread in the freezer. Let's see . . . one, two, three, four, five loaves. That should do it."

"You set the table and I'll start cooking."

"I think I hear our guests arriving."

"Yes, and they look famished. This ought to be a memorable dinner."

"There's only one problem," says your wife. "What are we going to do with all the leftovers?"

No one was thinking about leftovers when a horde of hungry people sat on a grassy mountainside for dinner. All four gospels record this celebrated story, the only miracle aside from the resurrection included by each of the writers. It begins when Jesus invites the apostles to a private retreat for a well-deserved break. "Come with me by yourselves to a quiet place and get some rest," he says (Mark 6:31). "So they went away by themselves in a boat to a solitary place" (v. 32).

Pause a moment to picture the next scene. Their boat lands on a desolate beach just after sunrise. The twelve prop chairs in the sand, take a load off, and gaze at the sea. Gentle waves lap the shore. Reflective conversation fills the air. Balmy temperatures accompany the soft breeze caressing their skin. Peter reaches into the YETI cooler and pulls out a frosty beverage. "Anyone thirsty?" Meanwhile, Jesus fires up the grill and cooks fish fillets over glowing coals. "Who's hungry?" Deep breaths, everyone. Deep breaths. Ahh! Relaxing, right?

Well, that's not how things go down. Not even close.

A crowd crashes their picnic and all the plans change.

Witnesses of Jesus' miracles craved more. And 5,000 of them (not counting women and children) trail Jesus like paparazzi on a deadline. When the masses show up, no bouncer fends them off. Jesus doesn't check IDs or inspect invitations. Everyone makes the guest list. The One who knows each person by name displays compassion. He welcomes them, heals them, teaches them. Afternoon arrives and it's obvious this crowd, growling tummies notwithstanding, plans to stick around for the afterglow.

In their remote location, no restaurants or food trucks can feed them. Grocery stores aren't an option. The apostles, with growing concern about eating arrangements, lobby Jesus to send the crowd to nearby towns. But the Bread of Life has a different notion. "You give them something to eat," says Jesus (Luke 9:13). Alrighty, then.

A boy with five loaves of barley (not five bread trucks) and two small fish (these weren't blue whales) provides ingredients for the meal. But how can so little feed so many? Will a spoonful of sand fill the Grand Canyon? Can a squirt gun douse a five-alarm fire? Are the coins in your child's piggy bank sufficient to satisfy our national debt?

Little goes far when God is involved. Not enough becomes plenty. A shortage becomes excess. Lack becomes abundance. Faith small as a mustard seed moves a mountain. Don't you love knowing a morsel of trust outweighs Mount Everest?

Jesus takes the bread and fish, looks to heaven, gives thanks, and breaks the loaves. The hands that once turned water into wedding wine now—with one sack of groceries—nourish thousands of hungry people. Everyone eats. All feel full. Was that a burp? The twelve disciples, on cleanup duty, pick up twelve baskets of leftovers. Yes, one dozen. A basket for each of them.

Why did Jesus feed the crowd? To show off? Win a bet? Prove someone wrong? Add another miracle to his burgeoning resume? Hardly.

Remember the birds.

Jesus likes to fill empty stomachs. He doesn't send people away hungry. The Satisfier says, "Whoever comes to me will never go hungry, and whoever believes in me will never be thirsty" (John 6:35). Dare to release your cares about basic needs. Dwell instead on his kingdom and righteousness. In this day and age, that requires focus.

Luke Aikins knows how to focus. He's a pilot, aerial photographer, and professional skydiver. And the first person to jump out of an airplane from the mid-tropospheric altitude of 25,000 feet without a parachute. On purpose. Needless to say, this was different than his 18,000 previous jumps.[5]

Racing to earth at 120 mph, it took 120 seconds to reach his target. What was he aiming for? An ocean? The world's largest trampoline? A football stadium filled with marshmallows? Nope. His landing pad was a 100-foot square net suspended 200 feet in the air designed to absorb the impact of his freefall. Had he missed the tiny target, well, let's just say no second chances.

Luke navigated his path using his hands to steer, somewhat like a ship's rudder. Tracking the drop zone from five miles high required sophisticated technology. GPS signals, emitted from Luke's helmet, guided his descent. A lighting system configured on the ground and visible from the sky flashed white when Luke advanced toward the target and red when he veered off course. White lights = life. Red lights = death.

I've never interviewed Luke, but I bet he stayed focused for those two adrenaline-pumping minutes. He wasn't thinking about dinner or wondering whether that men's suit he saw through the window at Macy's last week was on sale. He wasn't worried about his next mortgage payment or what the stock market was doing. His undivided attention was on his mission. Are the lights white or are they red? Am I on track or straying off course? White or red? *White* or *red*? For two breathtaking, heart-stopping, jaw-clenching minutes only one thing in the universe mattered to Luke Aikins.

Are the lights *white* or are they *red*?

Luke nailed the landing. The net did its job. The crowd went wild. Moments after hitting the bullseye, Mr. Aikins raised his hands in jubilation. "I'm almost levitating, it's incredible!"[6]

Mission accomplished.

Will you do a two-minute experiment with me? Set your timer. Ready? Go.

Draw one full measure of air into your lungs and hold it a few beats. Now exhale. Okay, visualize this scene: you're on a plane 25,000 feet in the air, cruising on autopilot. All of your financial baggage sits in the aircraft's cargo hold. This is the carry-on luggage that travels with you—whether you realize it or not—like sandspurs stuck to your shoelaces.

Every financial fear, care, concern, and worry. Last month's grocery receipts. A stack of bank statements. School tuition. Utility bills and car payments. The surgeon's invoice and hospital charges. Health insurance premiums (they went up again!?) and prescription drug payments. Retirement projections created by a wealth management advisor that considers income streams from your IRA, 401(k), social security, and pension plan. Oh, you don't have a pension plan? Right. That's noted on a memo buried somewhere in the pile.

The flight commander opens the bay doors. "Jump," he says. He's promised to guard the cargo hold until you touch down. You trust him. So you bail out, focus on your target, and navigate your path. For two free-falling minutes you forget about your financial baggage and enjoy the thrilling rush. What a feeling!

Now, what if two minutes could last a lifetime?

What if you were anxious for nothing, including money?

What if you traded worrisome thoughts for unwavering trust?

Instead of prioritizing your income statement, balance sheet, and retirement scenario, could seeking God's kingdom and righteousness be your first pursuits?

Yes, definitely. You can believe the Bird-Feeder. You can put your faith in the Flower-Clothier. The Good Shepherd cares for his flock. Isn't that priceless?

CHAPTER FIVE

◆ ◆ ◆

A DIRE WARNING

There are many things more precious than money.

EDDIE JAKU, AUTHOR OF THE HAPPIEST MAN ON EARTH,
THE BEAUTIFUL LIFE OF AN AUSCHWITZ SURVIVOR

I walked into an airport restroom recently and noticed a bold-faced, large-lettered sign permanently affixed to the wall, "CAUTION: Floor Might Be Wet." You couldn't miss it. My first thought: What else *might* the floor be? Coated with lava? Covered with marbles? Crawling with snakes? Could the floor, quite possibly, be clean and dry? Yes, thankfully. On that day, at that moment, my shoe soles contacted no hazardous substance.

We navigate a world where warnings abound, covering the spectrum from serious—DON'T TRY THIS AT HOME—to silly:

On a baby stroller: Caution—Remove Child Before Folding

On a bottle of dog medication: Warning—May Cause Drowsiness When Operating a car

On a "vanishing ink" marker: Notice—Should Not Be Used For Signing Checks or Any Legal Documents

On a cup of take-out coffee: Caution—Avoid Pouring On Lap

On a thermometer: Warning—Once Used Rectally The

Thermometer Should Not Be Used Orally[1]

True story. Our Nigerian Dwarf goats Mia (the brown one) and Belle (the black one) fell ill after eating azaleas in our yard. Guess how you take a goat's temperature? Correct... from the exhaust pipe, not the intake valve. At one point during their successful recovery period, I asked Mary Ann—she covers all animal maintenance at M & M Farm, "What happened to the thermometer? I think I have a fever and it's usually right here in the medicine cabinet."

"Oh," she nonchalantly replied, "I needed it for the goats. I figured I'd leave it down at the barn." Then she added with a wry smile, "Do you want me to go get it?"

We fell on the floor laughing.

Jesus issued warnings. Some about hell. Some about false teaching. But he also cautioned us about greed. "Watch out! Be on your guard against all kinds of greed; life does not consist in an abundance of possessions" (Luke 12:15). This doesn't appear to be a mere afterthought of helpful guidance, like: "Hey, the forecast calls for some rain today, might want to grab an umbrella." No. Jesus sounds serious. Other Bible translations use the words *beware* (NLT), *take heed* (KJV), *be careful* (ISV). It's like he's saying, "Don't slip, the floor isn't just wet, it's icy too."

Paul lists greed alongside other sins improper for God's holy people: wickedness, depravity, evil, envy, sexual immorality, slander, impurity, idolatry, murder, and malice (Rom. 1:29; 1 Cor. 6:9-10; Eph. 5:3). These evils hang out together and live in a dangerous neighborhood. Avoid the dark streets in this town.

He sounds another warning, one you've heard before (it's

often misquoted): "For the love of money is a root of all kinds of evil. Some people, eager for money, have wandered from the faith and pierced themselves with many griefs" (1 Tim. 6:10).

To be sure, money itself isn't the culprit. Money provides essentials for life. It buys time with friends and family. It grants freedom to pursue healthy interests. It can be given away to support noble causes. The problem arises when a voracious desire for money eclipses a passionate longing for God.

Greed craves more. It thirsts for another sip and hungers for one more bite. As Dallas Willard points out, "Human desire is infinite by nature; it cannot be satisfied."[2] Which reminds me of a potato chip commercial that aired in my youth. Their slogan? "Betcha' can't eat just one." They're correct, you can't. And when it comes to money and possessions, greed sees no finish line. "Whoever loves money never has money enough; whoever loves wealth is never satisfied with their income" (Eccles. 5:10). The insatiable nature of greed hoodwinks us. We think more of any "good" thing (money) is a blessing. But the Proverb writer knew better:

> ... give me neither poverty nor riches, but give
> me only my daily bread. Otherwise, I may have
> too much and disown you and say, 'Who is the
> Lord?' Or I may become poor and steal, and so
> dishonor the name of my God.
>
> (Prov. 30:8-9)

Of the three alternatives presented here—feast, famine, or just enough—which would you choose? It's easy to guess which one you're NOT picking.

Let's entertain a make-believe scenario that limits your options. A magic bottle washes ashore on the beach. You pick it up and smoke pours out. A genie materializes, holding neatly wrapped gift boxes topped with purple bows, one in each hand.

The genie nods toward the right, prompting you to lift the lid. The crimson suede interior protects a filigree scroll atop a bed of large diamonds. Once unrolled, the message reveals: *"You will spend the rest of your days in the Land of Luxury, with infinite riches available to fill every material desire you can imagine."* Very nice, you think, as your mind begins to fantasize about castles and kings, silk and satin. And a red Ferrari—trunk stuffed with cash, Rolex in the glove box, and the Hope Diamond as a hood ornament.

Then you shift your attention to the genie's left hand. With a tinge of hesitation, you remove the top from the second box. No suede or sparkles inside. Just flakes of rust encircling a square of stained parchment. As you read the note, goosebumps of giddiness turn into shivers of dread: *"You will spend the rest of your days in the Land of Poverty, where you'll scrimp, scrap, and beg for every morsel of food you raise to your mouth."* Hmm. Nothing appealing about that scene.

The genie awaits your decision, his preset options binary. You must choose one or the other, riches or poverty. What's your wish? Well, you've sorted through difficult choices before, but this makes front-page headlines in the *No-Brainer News*. You want the goose that lays golden eggs, the Midas touch, the richest-person-in-the-world title. Homeless destitution isn't your bag. Abject poverty isn't your fantasy. Rational people don't choose hunger and helplessness.

But ask yourself, will unlimited financial resources *really* make you happy?

Sudden wealth didn't give Shakespeare a better life. Not William Shakespeare. *Abraham* Shakespeare. He won a bundle in the Florida lottery in 2006, taking a lump-sum payout of $16.9 million. He wanted to share his winnings and help people, but as a largely illiterate laborer who lacked financial acumen, Abraham Shakespeare fell victim to schemers who preyed on his ignorance and innocence. The pressures of wealth took its toll. He felt isolated and lonely. He got mixed up with the wrong crowd. He told a childhood friend, "I thought all these people were my friends, but then I realized all they want is just money."[3]

Three years after Shakespeare's lottery dream came true, officials found his body buried nine feet deep under a concrete slab. What motivated the convicted murderer, Dee Dee Moore, his uncredentialed financial advisor, to commit the crime? Greed? Materialism? Love of money? That's my guess.

Just before he bought the winning ticket, Shakespeare was baptized and joined a church. But sadly, a friend noted, "When he won the lottery, he forgot about being saved."[4] Perhaps the proverb writer is right. Riches *can* take your mind off God.

Not everyone who comes into sudden wealth winds up doomed. Although many lottery winners unaccustomed to handling large sums of money squander their windfalls quickly, some exercise financial discipline and fare quite well. Nevertheless, a study surveying the well-being of Swedish lottery winners determined in spite of measured increases in life satisfaction experienced by some, their levels of overall happiness didn't change.[5] Money did not buy more happiness.

A priceless life—full of enjoyment, satisfaction, and purpose[6]—cannot be purchased at a department store. No online store sells authentic joy. No indulgence brings lasting happiness. Yet billions of marketing dollars are spent annually trying to persuade you otherwise. Hence, the problem. Misplaced desires fueled by (and this is ironic) companies greedy for your money perpetuate a cycle of unbridled consumption. (A shocking side note: Redirecting less than half of yearly advertising dollars spent luring consumers to buy the next gizmo, gadget, or indulgence would feed every hungry person in the world.)[7]

Jesus tells us it's all a mirage. An optical phenomenon. What you think you see isn't there. He warns against "all kinds of greed" (for the wrong things) because money, material possessions, power, worldly accomplishments—so many of the things we strive to obtain—won't satisfy our souls. The illusion resembles cotton candy. The pastel cloud of heaven carries an irresistible aroma. But adults know it's nothing more than a fluffy mass of sugar and air. It melts when your tongue touches it. No amount can ever nourish you. And it always leaves a sticky mess.

The kingdom of heaven is not Candyland. Deep in our hearts we want substance. Life that is truly life. And that comes only through loving, giving relationships with God and others.

It's foolish to crave things that leave us half-empty. Our king helps us recognize what's truly valuable with pithy back-to-back parables:

> The kingdom of heaven is like treasure hidden in
> a field. When a man found it, he hid it again, and

then in his joy went and sold all he had and
bought that field. Again, the kingdom of heaven is
like a merchant looking for fine pearls. When he
found one of great value, he went away and sold
everything he had and bought it.

(Matt. 13:44-46)

Jesus keeps it simple. But don't overlook the discovery process. Both the man and the merchant went looking for something. And these seekers found items of incomparable worth because that's how it is with Jesus. Seekers find. Askers get answers. Good gifts await curious souls who recognize a meaningful find when they see one.

Finding Forrest Fenn's treasure is a different story. In 2010, the eccentric eighty-year-old millionaire hid a chest containing gold, coins, and gems somewhere in the Rocky Mountains. He left clues to its whereabouts in a twenty-four-line poem entitled *The Thrill of the Chase*. For a decade, the bounty eluded tens of thousands of treasure hunters. The mystery was finally solved when thirty-two-year-old Michigan native Jack Stuef uncovered the loot buried somewhere in Wyoming.[8] It took him two years to find it. In the end, thousands of searchers came up empty-handed, and tragically, five people died on the quest.[9] Only one person won the prize. For whom was the thrill worth the chase?

If you seek what Jesus offers, you'll discover his riches, guaranteed. He won't play tricks, hide his fortunes, or lead you on a wild goose chase. Flashing neon arrows point the way. The critical part of the search comes at the end, as these parables indicate. A man finds a treasure, a merchant finds a pearl. And both make accurate appraisals of their joyful discoveries. Don't miss this! Both sold *all they had* to acquire something—one thing—worth *everything*. That's what the kingdom of heaven is like. Why would you settle for less?

And yet our striving continues. More. Bigger. Better. Faster.

You deserve it.

You're worth it.

You'll love it.

Gotta have it.

More toys. More clothes. More shoes. Bigger house. Built-in pool. Wider screen. Nicer car. Fatter paycheck. Season tickets. Speedboat. Getaway weekend. Exotic vacation. Tiffany jewelry. Coach purse. Second home. Third car. Four-wheeler. Five golden rings!

When is enough, enough?

Alas, it's the way we keep score, isn't it? What you drive. Where you live. How you dress. The world measures success by such things, temporal as they are. No thing lasts forever. Not even diamonds. The Greek word for diamonds is adamas, which means "unconquerable, invincible."[10] But under the right conditions, over time, diamonds can degrade into graphite. Which would transform a pair of two-carat earrings into very expensive pencils.

Your soul was made to live forever, but your stuff has a short shelf life.

When I was seventeen, I spent the summer working on the back of a garbage truck picking up trash. Old man Carl drove and I hung on for dear life. The Florida heat was brutal. It was nonstop, heavy labor for a 115-pound teenager, but I had a blast picking up bag after bag after bag (cans were seldom used back then). Got so good at slinging trash, if only one bag sat at the curb, Carl wouldn't stop the truck. He'd merely slow down, I'd grab the bag on the fly, swing it forward to gain momentum, then flip it around behind my back and into the hopper.

The only time I rested was when the truck filled up and we had to make the fifteen-mile trek to dump the load. My first visit to the landfill, well, let's just say it was a learning experience. I had never smelled that kind of smell before. Never seen mountains of rotting stuff. And what was up with all the seagulls? Years later, I reminisced about that memorable summer—I had proposed to Mary Ann that July and I knew she'd say yes . . . I was her Knight in Shining Garbage—and wrote a poem: *Ode To a Landfill.*

'Twas a trip to the landfill, and all I could see
Were piles of garbage, trash, and debris.
All of what once was so shiny and bright
Now is musty, dusty, covered with blight.

Washers, dryers, old 8-track tapes
Momma's broke vacuum, out-of-date drapes
Poppa's old Chevy, had four on the floor
Now here it sits—it don't run no more.

Furniture, hot tubs, computers, and clothes
iPods, snow skis, pot-bellied stoves.
All of the things that we once held so dear
Waste away, rust away, rot away here.

It's said, "One man's trash is another man's treasure"
But none of this junk will bring anyone pleasure.
The things we buy with the money we earn
When will we learn that it's all going to burn?

We'd be wise to stop loving money and material goods. They'll never love us back. They don't last. And they're not coming with us when we die. "We all come to the end of our lives as naked and empty-handed as on the day we were born. We can't take our riches with us" (Eccles. 5:15 NLT). Every person on the *Forbes* list of billionaires is going out broke.

Like Jesus, Paul knew money-lovers would get into trouble. It comes with the territory. Old Testament Achan serves as a dramatic example. Greed fueled his disobedience. In the battle of Jericho, he took for himself spoils that belonged in the Lord's treasury. When confronted, he confessed.

> It's true. I sinned against God, the God of Israel.
> This is how I did it. In the plunder I spotted a
> beautiful Shinar robe, two hundred shekels of
> silver, and a fifty-shekel bar of gold, and I coveted
> and took them. They are buried in my tent with
> the silver at the bottom.
>
> (Josh. 7:20-21 THE MESSAGE)

Achan's picture should be posted next to the verse, "The greedy bring ruin to their households" (Prov. 15:27). His sin cost the lives of thirty-six soldiers, his entire family, and his own. The pile of stones that killed him marks his grave.

In both the Old and New Testaments, from Achan to

Zacchaeus (the tax collector who met Jesus and subsequently repented of his thievery), the Bible records stories of "all kinds of evil" catalyzed by greed. We need not catalog each act. But we must stand guard.

Because of the love of money, even God-fearing, law-abiding citizens sometimes act of out character. They get too creative preparing tax returns. Fudge the truth to make a sale. Hide assets while filing for bankruptcy. Make risky bets to get rich quick. Some end up humiliated, imprisoned, or steeped in debt. Some lose their faith. Some lose their families. And as we have seen, some end up dead.

Are the dire warnings any wonder? Paul wasn't kidding. Jesus isn't joking. "No one can serve two masters. Either you will hate the one and love the other, or you will be devoted to the one and despise the other. You cannot serve both God and money" (Matt. 6:24). With these provocative words, Jesus throws down the gauntlet. His clear ultimatum: it's one or the other. Choose you must, there's no fence to straddle.

Perhaps this marks a poignant, or even painful, moment. You're divided because you desire to serve God, not money, but you fear part of your heart—some hidden chamber—isn't up to the challenge. Past actions indict you. Failings convict you. You've been tempted and trapped, sucked in and snared. How can you live up to this expectation? Could an enchanted genie offer assistance?

Don't be silly. Of course not.

But the Holy Spirit can.

On your not-yet-fully-sanctified journey, he's along for the ride as your inside guide. The Holy Spirit can power you through the pull of opposing pursuits. He welcomes his role of directing, strengthening, and encouraging you on this pilgrimage. Can you sense his presence, feel his warmth, trust his promptings? I hope so. Our Holy Spirit is here, now.

Use your imagination, and look deeply, closely, there in his hands. It's a bewildering, marvelous sight! A golden bowl overflowing with grace. Such surprising beauty, unexpected and undeserved. Keep breathing. Pay attention. Stay in the moment. Is this how Moses felt when the bush burned?

He extends his arms so you can see the silver key deep inside the bowl of grace. Gleaming light dances off its edges. *A key? Why a key? Where's the lock?* But wait, something else . . . *is that a scroll?* Ah, indeed. An ancient, brittle, mysterious scroll!

Our Holy Spirit gestures. *Handle with care,* you tell yourself, *this scroll looks older than the angel Gabriel.* Patiently, you unspool the secret message. A few specks of vellum flake off the edges, but the fragile document unrolls unharmed. The blood-red letters want to be seen and with eyebrows raised you read the words:

> *In my kingdom, it is more blessed to give than to*
> *receive. I created you to live and love in my*
> *abundance. But danger lurks. Greed sabotages your*
> *desire to be generous. Love of money leads you*
> *astray. Both inflict untold harm and at times you*
> *feel powerless under their spell. But take courage.*
> *Choose wisely. Follow me. Be of good cheer. This*
> *silver key will unshackle your heart from the love of*
> *money and bondage of greed. A priceless life—in all*

its freedom and fullness—beckons. My blessings are
yours, now and forever.

A strange euphoria engulfs your spirit. But you're puzzled. The lock? Where is the lock that pairs with the key? What box, what safe, what door does it open?

In the midst of these perplexing questions, a pleasant aroma, like cinnamon with a faint touch of honey, drifts from the bowl. The key is now glowing and warm to the touch. Carefully, delicately, you pick it up and notice the inscriptions.

One word is engraved on the front: Contentment.

And a single word on the back: Gratitude.

A slow moment passes. Then a revelation illuminates your being. Of course! That's the answer! In silence, you ponder the key that will unlock your priceless life.

CHAPTER SIX

◆ ◆ ◆

SOMETHING'S MISSING

*He who is not contented with what he has,
would not be contented with what he would like to have.*

SOCRATES

*O*ur first four cows arrived already named: Maggie, Ruby, Annie, and Daisy. The ladies adjusted quickly to their new environment. Double the fenced pasture as their previous home and blanketed in green grass, it's a veritable salad bar—a Garden of Eatin'. The grazing creatures munch on lush vegetation and drink fresh, cool water. That could be why Maggie, Ruby, and Annie always seem merry. But then there's Daisy.

Like all herd animals, cattle tend to stick together for social and safety reasons. They enjoy each other's company and are smarter than most people suspect. Our cows understand the four strands of flexible wire running the perimeter of our pasture form the boundaries of their turf. If they get too close to the fence, a pulse of electricity reminds them to maintain a friendly buffer. And they all keep their distance. Except Daisy.

Daisy fell for the oldest trick in the devil's book. Literally. She wanted something different, something more, something better. Something other than the ample provisions and happy family life she already enjoyed. So Daisy learned to lift (and endure the shocks of) the electric wire with her horns, sneak under it, and move her 1,000-pound body into the field where our farmhouse sits. Perhaps the grass looked greener on the other side of the fence. Trust me, it's not. Daisy was deceived.

Humanity's first instance of deception was sown through seeds of discontentment. The familiar story takes place in a paradisical garden where sin is absent. No disease, no pestilence, no war. No suffering, murder, or theft. No high blood pressure, heart attacks, acne, or Alzheimer's. Depression and anxiety don't exist. Divorces and lawsuits aren't filed. It's a land of perfect harmony and unspoiled peace. The Creator walks in creation with his created ones. All is well in Eden. The grass has never been greener.

Until the serpent speaks.

In the book of Genesis, this event follows Adam and Eve's wedding ceremony. How soon after God invited Adam to kiss the bride did the reptile slither onto the scene? Did he crash the reception, pretending to be a friend? Were the newlyweds able to enjoy a honeymoon? We don't know. But the clever deceiver has a knack for timing.

The fall of mankind begins with a question. "Did God really say...?" It doesn't matter what words come next, does it? The trap is set. Satan raises doubt, knocking Eve off balance. He continues, "... you must not eat from any tree in the garden?" (Gen. 3:1). Eve corrects the serpent, telling him the only tree off-limits grows in the middle of the garden. That one will kill us; the others are fine. The fraudster answers the woman: "You will not certainly die, ... For God knows that when you eat from it your eyes will be opened, and you will be like God, knowing good and evil" (v. 4–5).

The banned produce seems nutritious. Aesthetically, it's beautiful. Best of all, it unlocks superpowers. This forbidden fruit hits the trifecta of worldly cravings: lust of the flesh, lust of the eyes, and pride of life (1 John 2:16). Eve plucks a piece off the tree, opens her mouth, takes a bite, and swallows. She hands it to Adam and he joins in the fruit fest. With that, all hell breaks loose. In one defining moment, the course of history jumps the tracks.

How did Satan lure Eve into sin? What did the devil do to provoke disobedience? The same thing he does today. Our adversary claims, "Something's missing." Something different. Something more. Something better. Whatever you have, it's not enough. God's holding out on you.

Contentment (or lack of) extends far beyond the realm of money. The author of Hebrews offers sage advice, "Keep your life free from the love of money and be content with what you have..." (Heb. 13:5). Money ranks high on the list of things we desire; however, our unsatisfied nature knows no bounds. Beyond money, we yearn for status and attention. We seek power, prestige, pleasure, possessions. *See who I am. See what I know. See what I've done. See what I have.*

These sins of pride fuel unhealthy comparison and ungodly competition. Our obsessed culture measures, ranks, grades, and counts. We sort, separate, select and classify. We create top-to-bottom lists and categorization systems which create awareness of where we stand compared to our peers. And ordinary won't cut it. By definition, average is nothing special. We feel better about ourselves... when we think we're better than others.

Nobody wants to be a nobody.

Consider your emotional response to this hypothetical Q&A with a couple of different answer options:

Q: What's your I.Q.?

    A. I don't like to brag, but they say I'm a genius.

    B. I'm in the lowest quartile of the bell curve, whatever that means.

Q: Did your grandson make the starting lineup on the all-star baseball squad?

    A. Yes, he pitches and bats cleanup, too.

    B. No. He never made it off the bench in the recreational league.

Q: Where is your child going to college?

    A. She's been accepted to Harvard, Yale, and Stanford. Still hasn't decided.

    B. Her test scores aren't high enough for college.

Q: What do you do for a living?

    A. I'm CEO of my own multimillion dollar business.

    B. I'm unemployed. Can't find a decent job in this town.

Q: Can you tell me about your favorite vacation?

    A. Well, I've traveled to all seven continents, so it's hard to pick my favorite trip.

    B. I've never been out of my home state.

If choice "B" resembles your real-life answer to one of these questions (or any of a thousand others similar in nature), you likely don't feel good about it. Why? Because although this world is not our home, we can't help but adopt its values. Too often, we care more about what people think than what God thinks. Yet the instant you see God face-to-face, it is doubtful he'll ask how many votes you got for the high school homecoming court. He's not worried about who was named class president, most-likely-to-succeed, or MVP of the sports team.

God knows mathematically speaking, for every category conjured up, half of his beloved image-bearers land in the below-average group. But the world's classification construct is utterly irrelevant. What really matters are items of eternal significance. Your relationship with him, and others, supersedes cultural obsessions. Maybe that's why the verse, "Keep your life free from the love of money and be content with what you have . . ." ends like this: ". . . because God has said, 'Never will I leave you; never will I forsake you'" (Heb. 13:5). God wants you to know he's near, always. And the Hebrews writer wants you to know God's relational presence matters more than money. Or anything else.

The truth is easy to forget when you experience failure or don't measure up to the world's standards. You feel like a sad-faced emoji when some statistic places you in the bottom bracket and you're not second best, you're least best. Who wants to be the last one picked, runt of the litter, a rotten apple?

When you're missing out and left out, it can leave you down and out, checking out. These feelings of inferiority don't inspire satisfaction and happiness. Instead, they foster a lack of contentment, prompting you to seek something different, something more, something better. And an inward, self-serving focus can mean eternally weighty matters—including generously meeting the needs of others—fade into the background.

A parable about a farmer sowing seed illustrates this reality by describing the potential efficacy of God's word in four different soil types. Jesus explains: Seeds falling on a path are quickly stolen by Satan; seeds sprinkled on rocky places form no permanent roots. Both lead to unfruitful outcomes. Skip to the fourth soil condition, seeds sown on good soil. Here a person hears the word, accepts it, and produces a bumper crop. Bingo, that's the goal. Unfortunately, the third scenario—seeds among thorns—is far too common.

> Still others, like seed sown among thorns, hear the word; but the worries of this life, the deceitfulness of wealth, and the desires for other things come in and choke the word, making it unfruitful.
>
> (Mark 4:18-19)

Can you relate? You're minding your own business when the world knocks on your door. "Knock, knock."

"Who's there?"

A greener pasture. A piece of fruit with supernatural powers. A new, slinky dress. A set of steak knives that can cut through concrete. A résumé-building career opportunity with a bigger paycheck, but also more stress, less sleep, poor health, and family sacrifices. A program that promises to catapult your kid to the top of the class. A special edition, levitating iPhone that takes perfect selfies of you in ideal situations (yes, your hair looks amazing!) and posts them on social media with autogenerated captions written to maximize "likes."

Take that, junior-high bully who called me a loser. How do you like me now?

Meanwhile, the word of God gets strangled.

That which is intended to infuse life and provide direction will have to wait. Other priorities beckon. The living, breathing, life-changing word—unheeded and unwanted—struggles for oxygen. Hook up the ventilator. Put God's word on life support. Lack of contentment is choking it to death.

I know what it's like to lack contentment. You see, I'm what Barry Schwartz, author of *The Paradox of Choice*, calls a *maximizer*. Maximizers "seek and accept only the best."[1] In contrast, a *satisficer* settles for good enough. Satisficers don't fret about the possibility that there might be something better out there.

I strive for perfection and need assurance that every decision I make, out of all known (and sometimes unknown) possibilities, is the optimal one. Sounds noble, even godly, right? When choosing a spouse or facing a moral dilemma, yes. But when trying to decide what's for dinner, what to wear to the gym, or which of the sixty-seven varieties of toothpaste on the grocer's shelves is just right for my pearly whites, no.

When taken to extremes and applied in inconsequential situations, the maximizer nature is draining. A maximizer expends finite mental resources playing the comparison game in a world with infinite choices. I understand why Teddy Roosevelt said, "Comparison is the thief of joy." A brain on high alert never rests. If every decision—even a trivial one—needs to be perfect, discontentment is inevitable.

All that to say: When a spirit of discontentment colonizes my mind,[2] even God's powerful word has difficulty breaking through. Thorny soil rules the day. Worries of this life weigh me down. Deceitfulness of wealth sucks me in. Desire for other things sweeps me away. Nothing's actually missing, but I'm still searching.

I'm acting like Daisy.

When I find myself loitering in the *"Something's Missing"* zone, I remember Russell Conwell's *Acres of Diamonds* lecture. The Temple University founder delivered the same speech, about a prosperous Persian farmer who catches wind of an alluring legend, over 6,000 times. There are diamond fields out there somewhere, just waiting to be discovered. And it's finders keepers.

Intrigue overcomes the ambitious farmer. He abandons his fertile pastures, productive as they are, to seek a fortune certain to multiply his riches. Far and wide he travels. Sunrise to sunset he searches. Night after night he dreams. But every day of this challenging journey ends empty. Many years pass, and no stones of opulence are found.

As fate would have it, the mythical diamonds are discovered soon after the farmer's death. Acres of them. Can you guess their secret hiding place? Yes, right on his own soil. The poor man spent a lifetime searching for the very thing he unknowingly possessed. Conwell's lesson: "Your diamonds are not in far distant mountains or in yonder seas; they are in your own backyard, if you but dig for them."[3]

Could it be that everything you're longing for is already in your possession?

It might not be as simple (or trivial) as finding the car keys you're frantically searching for in the front pocket of the pants you're wearing. Or realizing the sunglasses you can't locate are right on top of your head. Sometimes you have to dig. It might take a little work. Grass is greener where you water it.

It's important to understand contentment isn't synonymous with complacency. Nor is it an apathetic, I—don't—care—about—anything attitude. There is a time to stay put and a time to saddle up. When you identify a gap between who you are and who you want to be (or what you have and what you think you want), ask yourself: Is this a "true, noble, right, pure, lovely, and admirable" pursuit (Phil. 4:8), or an exercise to resurrect my fading glory, keep up with the Joneses, or gain fifteen minutes of fame?

Once you're convinced your motives are honorable, move forward. Press on toward the target. Then realize *before* you hit all your ambitious goals, get what you "want," awaken the giant within, and reach your full potential, it's possible to live in a state of contentment just as you currently are.

But how, you ask, can I be content when something vital is missing in my life?

When every time one deficiency gap closes, another opens wide?

When after I get what I want, I often don't want what I got?

When I still roam like Daisy and search like the Persian farmer?

Great questions.

You're ready to learn Paul's secret and meet David's shepherd.

While imprisoned in Rome (likely under house arrest), the apostle Paul wrote a short letter to the Philippian Christians. In this note, expressions of joy occur no less than sixteen times. Near the end of the epistle Paul declares, "I have learned to be content whatever the circumstances." (Phil. 4:11). Acknowledging he knows what it's like to be in need as well as have plenty, Paul repeats himself, "I have learned the secret of being content in any and every situation . . ." (v. 12). The *secret*?

This elusive secret remains a mystery to most. Understanding differential calculus, mastering Mandarin Chinese, or learning to play the French horn seem easier than learning how to be content. But Paul claims he's cracked the code.

Paul . . . struck blind at his conversion. Paul . . . shipwrecked, stoned, and snakebitten. Paul . . . flogged on five occasions and beaten thrice. Paul didn't travel smooth roads or sleep on soft pillows. Danger followed him like a dark shadow. He'd have never qualified for life insurance.

Chronicling his extensive sufferings in a second letter to the Corinthians, he saved the worst for last: a tormenting affliction described as a thorn in the flesh, a messenger of Satan. Scholars don't agree on the diagnosis, but the ailment caused Paul so much pain he pleaded with God to take it away. Not once. Not twice. But three times.

When was the last time you pleaded with God, repeatedly?

What's the thorn in your flesh?

What are you desperate to wave goodbye to?

Failures and fears? Panic attacks? Bouts of hypochondria? An overbearing boss, inattentive spouse, or unruly child? An addiction you can't shake or loneliness you don't understand? Surely you struggle with something, or soon will. Thorns live on the stem of life.

Our tender God answered Paul's desperate prayer. The answer, however, was no. *No, Paul, I won't remove the thorn in your flesh.* What? *No?* Doesn't persistent prayer pay off? You'd think God would give Paul a break. The guy planted churches and preached to kings. He wrote a significant chunk of the New Testament. Who's done more to advance the gospel than Paul? Why in the world would God refuse him?

One reason: God had something better in mind.

It's called grace.

God told Paul, "My grace is sufficient for you, for my power is made perfect in weakness" (2 Cor. 12:9). That's that. Paul took God at his word. He made a deliberate choice to embrace the thorn, accept his hardships, and rely on the strength God's grace provided.

How much grace do you need today? A teaspoon, a cup, or a barrel? Worry not. God will soak you in seven oceans of sparkling grace if that's what it takes to settle your soul. Paul had his troubles and you have yours. And what God did for Paul he'll do for you. Trust in his grace. There's always enough to fill the gap.

Sufficient grace was part of Paul's secret to contentment. But even more so—the bigger picture—was the full measure of Christ himself. Christ gave Paul "I-can-do-all-things" strength. Not to cross an ocean or climb a giant sequoia, but to experience contentment no matter the circumstances. That's why Paul wanted Christ more than anything. More than health, wealth, or prosperity. More than status, standing, or worldwide fame. To Paul, Christ plus nothing was everything and everything without Christ was nothing.

New Testament Paul, the tentmaker, understood what Old Testament David, the shepherd-king, knew 1,000 years before him.

The Lord is sufficient.

David put it this way: "The Lord is my Shepherd, I lack nothing" (Ps. 23:1).

Is this the best opening line in the entire Psalm collection? David the shepherd-king sings of his own Shepherd-King. His confident words indicate who he trusts for provision, protection, and direction. Green pastures? Check. Quiet waters? Check. Soul restoration? Check. The benefits don't stop there, but David's first words capture the point. Because the Lord is his shepherd, nothing's missing. Everything the sheep needs, the sheep gets.

You have a shepherd, too. And a king. Your shepherd is who or what you follow, trust, and depend on. Your king is who or what you worship, serve, and are ruled by. The world offers plenty of options in many forms. But these pseudo-shepherds and pseudo-kings can't satisfy you like the Lord, because no one and nothing loves you the same way (or ever will). End of story.

When you are content in Christ, you can stop staring in the mirror and start looking out the window. "Do not merely look out for your own personal interests, but also for the interests of others" (Phil. 2:4 NASB). You can be generous beyond your wildest dreams, because for you, nothing's missing.

CHAPTER SEVEN

◆ ◆ ◆

THREE WORDS

Give thanks to the Lord, for he is good.
His love endures forever.

PSALM 136:1

*D*o you remember who spoke at Gettysburg? Besides Abraham Lincoln? It was the distinguished Edward Everett, Harvard professor and popular orator who delivered a splendid two-hour lecture extolling the virtues of national supremacy. Immediately after the 13,607-word speech, Honest Abe took the podium and uttered a mere 272 words.[1] His Gettysburg Address stands as one of the most famous speeches in American history.

Afterwards, Mr. Everett confessed to Lincoln, "I wish that I could flatter myself that I had come as near to the central idea of the occasion, in two hours, as you did in two minutes."[2] Ever the gentleman, Lincoln wrote back to Everett the next day offering sincere compliments for his valuable discourse.[3]

When you're trying to get a message across, how many words does it take? Perhaps it depends on the person. Maybe it depends on the setting. Either way, if you want to express gratitude it does not need to get complicated. Speak thousands if you wish, hundreds if it suits you. But three simple words will suffice.

Thank you, Lord.

It's not the quantity of words that matter, it's the sincerity with which we say them. "Thank you" conveys the sentiment; "Lord" indicates to whom we're giving thanks.

How often do these three words spring off your tongue?

And when are you most likely to say them?

Oftentimes, gratitude is a spontaneous internal reaction that occurs when we're delivered from immediate crisis or chronic distress. The fever subsides. The prodigal child returns. The sea parts. The rain comes. What sweet relief!

Turbulence turns to smooth air and breathing returns to normal. *Thank you, Lord.*

Your estranged spouse resolves to make the marriage work. *Thank you, Lord.*

The widespread layoffs, you're told, won't affect you. *Thank you, Lord.*

The inebriated driver blowing through the red light misses broadsiding your SUV by a millisecond. *Thank you, Lord.*

When you feel it, say it.

Nine of ten lepers healed by Jesus didn't. In biblical times, leprosy was a disease nobody wanted. The incurable ailment disfigured skin and twisted limbs. Hands curled into claws, nerve endings dulled, lesions formed, faces deformed.[4] To make matters worse, because early Israelites believed the illness was punishment for sin, along with physical suffering came social ostracism.[5] Lepers were shunned. Get used to the sidelines. Forget about friend requests. Don't expect to pull party invitations out of the mailbox.

When these ten outcasts met Jesus along the border between

Samaria and Galilee, they kept their distance and called out loudly, "Jesus, Master, have pity on us" (Luke 17:13). In a twist, Jesus doesn't heal them immediately. "When he saw them he said, 'Go show yourselves to the priests.' And as they went, they were cleansed" (v. 14). That's when you'd assume all ten jumped for joy like uncaged kangaroos.

Consider your reaction if you were wrapped in their robes. Stricken by a horrible malady. Exiled from society. No escape from the suffering. With nothing to lose, you take a chance on the gentle Galilean. Why not? As you scurry off to the religious leaders, hoping for the best but not expecting much, your fingers untwist and toes begin tingling.

Dead nerves come to life. Warm sensations replace cold numbness. Scales flake off your healing skin. Scabs disappear, scars flatten out, and a smile forms on your unfrozen face. Astonished, you pinch yourself. Nope, not a dream.

What is it like to laugh through tears? Every cell in your body cheers with glee. Are you grateful? C'mon. Of course, you are. How could the same not be so for these ten? But only one turned back to thank the healer.

A single loud voice that earlier begged for mercy now shouts praises to God. "He threw himself at Jesus' feet and thanked him—and he was a Samaritan" (v. 16). Jesus appears puzzled. Wait, what? "Were not all ten cleansed? Where are the other nine? Has no one returned to give praise to God except this foreigner?" (v. 17–18).

The nine, no doubt, had places to go and people to see. Cured, yes, but still under quarantine until the priests officially pronounced them clean. Hence, their hurry. The declaration granted permission to rejoin public life. They could return to their wives and children and friends and synagogues.[6] Imagine the reunions! How happy they were! But wait. Do you sense the one who thanked Jesus was happier still? "Rise and go," says Jesus, "your faith has made you well" (v. 19). Free to carry on like the nine, but with a heart gladdened all the more. Simply from saying, *Thank you, Lord.*

It's one thing to have thoughts of thanks and another to tangibly express them. If you feel something, say something. When we thank God, we praise God. The two acts are hitched together like horse and buggy:

- "Enter his gates with thanksgiving and his courts with praise; give thanks to him and praise his name" (Ps. 100:4).

- "I thank and praise you, O God of my ancestors . . ." (Dan. 2:23).

- "Now, our God, we give you thanks, and praise your glorious name" (1 Chron. 29:13).

Maybe that's why the Bible tells us to be thankful in *all* circumstances, not just when we're delivered from dread. For "this is God's will for you in Christ Jesus" (1 Thes. 5:18). As William Law noted hundreds of years ago, "If one cannot thank and praise God as well in calamities and suffering as in prosperity and happiness, how can such an attitude be called a real trust in God at all?[7] Henri Nouwen expands the idea, "True gratitude embraces all of life: the good and the bad, the joyful and the painful, the holy and the not-so-holy."[8]

Are you anxious? I get it. Fret no more. "Do not be anxious about anything, but in every situation, by prayer and petition, *with thanksgiving*, present your requests to God" (Phil. 4:6, emphasis mine). Have you ever forgotten to give thanks while pleading for relief? You're not alone. When I omit the "give thanks" element from my foxhole prayers, I firmly believe God still hears me. However, when I soak my petitions *with thanksgiving*, soothing peace always arrives sooner.

Are you suffering? Who hasn't suffered? Count your blessings anyway. Short of breath and riddled with cancer, eighty-year-old Oliver Sacks knew death lurked near. His response:

> I cannot pretend I am without fear. But my predominant feeling is one of gratitude. I have loved and been loved; I have been given much and I have given something in return; I have read and traveled and thought and written.[9]

Are you stuck between a rock and a hard place? We've all been there. Say, *Thank you, Lord.* "Consider it pure joy, my brothers and sisters, whenever you face trials of many kinds, because you know that the testing of your faith produces perseverance" (James 1:2–3).

Take in the testimony of a woman diagnosed with Stage 4 breast cancer. After processing the news, Lisa determined to move forward with gratitude: "Being thankful changed my heart. It changed my perspective. I'm just thankful for today." Seven years after the diagnosis, her husband Stuart remarked, "Gratitude has been our constant companion."[10]

Are you celebrating? Does all feel right in your world? What a great time to give thanks! Savor the moment. Soak in sunbeams. Shout Hallelujah! More than 2,700 scripture passages use the words *joy, happiness, gladness, merriment, pleasure, cheer, laughter, delight, jubilation, feasting, exultation, and celebration.*[11] That's even more than the 2,300 verses related to money![12] Our happy God loves it when we rejoice in him and give thanks to him.

Gratitude begins when we recognize, remember, and reflect on our blessings. Big things, little things, all things. The Milky Way galaxy, happy teardrops, and an infinite number of other miracles.

It's winter at the Grand Canyon. I rest on a rim-side bench and survey rock ledges decorated with snow. Did angels sprinkle powdered sugar on these canyon walls? White frosting tops plateaus. Purity. Stillness. Serenity. No camera can capture the splendor. Oh, the vast glory of it all! The closing verse in Psalms floods my mind, "Let everything that has breath, praise the Lord. Praise the Lord" (Ps. 150:6). As if on cue, a sudden drumming noise interrupts my tranquil worship. I spin around and spot a common woodpecker pounding his beak on a Ponderosa Pine not fifty feet away. Is he calling a mate? Or, in his own language, praising the Lord? With blue sky above and fresh snow below, wherever I look marvels abound. Big things, little things, all things. Words fail me. I whisper, *Thank you, Lord.*

Don't overlook the source of your blessings. Lucky stars have nothing to do with them. Good fortune hasn't singled you out. Every good gift comes from the Giver. He chooses, wraps, and delivers the lot of them. That's why we sing, "Praise God (not our lucky stars) from whom *all* blessings flow." Big blessings, little blessings, every blessing. Even the ones not on our gift registry. The challenging ones dressed as unsolvable problems or disguised as unwanted circumstances.[13] The ones prompting the question, "Why me?" The ones that knock you into a rut that feels like a circular trench.[14]

Have you been blessed with a blessing you didn't request?

You wanted a partner. Not an abusive relationship.

You prayed to get pregnant. Didn't ask for the miscarriage.

You sought a promotion. Now the company owns you seven days a week and treats you like a piece of machinery.

You hoped to grow old with the love of your life. Dementia wasn't part of your golden-years plan.

A diving accident left Joni Erickson Tada paralyzed from the shoulders down at just seventeen years old. A season of doubt, depression, and anger ensued. But the grief didn't last. Decades later, Joni acknowledged the life-changing event felt like a horrible tragedy in the beginning, but now she says:

> I give thanks *in* my wheelchair . . . I'm grateful *for* my quadriplegia. It's a bruising of a blessing. A gift wrapped in black. It's the shadowy companion that walks with me daily, pulling and pushing me into the arms of my Savior. And *that's* where the joy is.[15]

Joni found joy in her wheelchair. A spirit of thankfulness shapes her being. Her resilient spirit has infected others. In her long lifetime, she's inspired countless people through her art, writings, songs, and attitude.

You can't overestimate the power of gratitude. Some deem it the healthiest of all human emotions.[16] Roman philosopher Cicero believed gratitude to be not only the greatest of virtues but the parent of all others. Imagine it as the seed to a thousand flower gardens. Or the trunk of the Virtue Tree, sprouting branches adorned with leaves of wisdom, humility, courage, justice, respect, forgiveness, and every fruit of the Spirit.

Gratitude fends off destructive emotions. When negative feelings of "envy, greed, hostility, worry, irritation, resentment (we could go on)"[17] bite like a rattlesnake, gratitude serves as antivenom. Grateful people tend to be less materialistic, less depressed, less lonely. They're more pleasant to be around, more likely to help others in need, and better able to manage stress.[18]

Numerous studies link expressions of gratitude to positive mental and physical health. "Behavior changes biology."[19] Giving thanks releases bundles of happy hormones, like oxytocin, dopamine, and serotonin.[20] These chemicals trigger a surprise party in your brain. Pin up the streamers. Toss the confetti. Strike up the band. Say, *Thank you, Lord.*

It's not happiness that brings us gratitude. It's gratitude that brings us happiness.[21]

If gratitude came in pill form, I'm sure it'd be widely prescribed. You'd find a bottle in my medicine cabinet and a case in my closet. They could make a chewable version and call them Gratitude Gumdrops.

You know the list of adverse side effects that accompanies many prescription drugs?

Don't drink, don't drive, don't smoke, don't eat. May cause

dizziness, drowsiness, anxiety, or depression. May result in high blood pressure, headaches, or ringing in the ears. May trigger an itchy rash, scratchy throat, dry mouth, or constipation. May induce insomnia . . . or sudden death!

Umm. No thanks. A bad reaction to the cure could be worse than the current condition. But there would be no downside to Gratitude Gumdrops. Picture the label:

- Zero harmful side effects.
- Safe to use while driving.
- Recommended by 10 out of 10 doctors.
- As effective for toddlers as it is for seniors.
- May cause unexplainable happiness.
- Noticeably affects the way others are drawn to you.
- Likely adds years to your life; definitely adds life to your years.
- Widespread benefits linger longer than expected.
  I like those side effects.

Sometimes science confirms experimentally what you already know intuitively. Doesn't savoring life lift your mood? Aren't coping skills sharper when you appreciate your circumstances, whatever they may be? Can we agree relationships improve when you tell people they matter? Could you imagine any friend or physician, counselor or cleric, saying, "The answer to your problems is to be less grateful?" Not likely.

Which feels better: naming blessings or complaining about troubles? As gratefulness increases, grumbling decreases. When this happens in my home (translation: when I stop griping and start practicing gratitude) everyone's happier, including the dog.

Dogs naturally tend to be grateful creatures. Our Golden Retriever, Myleigh, sticks by my side like gum on a shoe. She's old enough to collect social security and totally deaf. But I watch Myleigh limp with a smile on her face. I see her joy as she struggles up the porch steps. I can't stop her kisses while I brush her matted fur. As a Golden Retriever in her golden years, retrieving is rare for her but tail wagging isn't. When gobbling up a treat, her body language shouts: "Thank you, thank you, thank you. I'm so very, very *happy!*"

Just as doggy gratitude can't keep its tail still, human gratitude can't keep its mouth shut, hands tied, or heart contained. Gratitude needs an outlet like a teapot needs a spout. Thankfulness builds within us, then bursts out in joyful praise. What's more, heart-full gratitude inspires hand-opening generosity.

A pastor friend shared the contents of an offering envelope collected on a recent weekend. Nineteen dollars sat tucked inside. A note on the back read:

> *Going through a divorce. Attorney fees just to keep my home is taking every spare cent. But this is all the cash from my wallet. It won't cover anything but maybe coffee for the breakroom. I pray God multiplies this abundantly for the church and his people. Thank you for such beautiful services.*

On that Sunday, a moment of gratitude led to a gesture of generosity. What if moments like this became lifetime habits for all of us? Oh, what a wonderful world it would be!

We speak of big hearts, but content matters more than size.

A.A. Milne wrote tales about lovable characters and their delightful escapades in the children's classic, *Winnie-the-Pooh*. One line he penned convicts me: "Piglet noticed that even though he had a Very Small Heart, it could hold a rather large amount of Gratitude."

How much gratitude does *your* heart hold?

Nineteen dollars' worth?

Enough to fill the Grand Canyon?

The amount it would take to find joy in a wheelchair?

Like Piglet, your heart possesses a high capacity for gratitude. This, too, is a gift from God. But you must unwrap this gift to enjoy its benefits. So, this is your wakeup call. You have a homework assignment: Relish the countless wonders of life and ponder your blessings, one by one. Don't hurry. You've got lots of ground to cover.

How could God be so good to you?

Why does he love you so dearly?

What are the ways he's shown it?

When you answer these questions, gratitude surges. You'll feel a spring of life fill your heart and stream through your veins. May the experience so move you that these three words become your daily anthem of praise: *Thank you, Lord.* For big things, little things, all things. Especially your priceless life.

CHAPTER EIGHT

◆ ◆ ◆

IT'S GOING TO COST YOU

I will not sacrifice to the Lord
my God burnt offerings that cost me nothing.

2 SAMUEL 24:24

*C*has Crutchfield loved his candy apple red 1969 Mach 1 Mustang. It was "one of one." No other car rolled off Ford's assembly line that year with its exact specifications. Chas found the vehicle in a neighbor's barn and spent three years restoring it to showroom condition. The meticulous work consumed him. No shortcuts or substitutes allowed. Every bolt and nut on the 429 Cobra Jet engine had to match the originals. The white interior needed to shine like it did in '69. The AM/FM radio had to play Rolling Stones' songs the same way they sounded when Neil Armstrong first stepped on the moon.

When Chas finished the project and cruised down Main Street, it wasn't only classic car lovers turning their heads to admire the vintage Mustang. Who doesn't enjoy an authentic piece of American nostalgia? Henry Ford grinned from his grave.

Not long after Chas put away the wrenches and swept up his shop, the rural church he attended started a fundraising initiative to build a new children's wing. Chas began praying. He heard his pastor talk about hope for future generations and wanted to participate in a meaningful way. But his appetite to contribute surpassed the balance in his bank account. Still, he prayed. And he sensed God's spirit prodding him to do something so crazy it prompted an investigation. He auctioned off the car and gave every cent to the church.

But wait, there's more. Chas also donated his MAKO fishing boat and an almost new, fully customized AR-15 rifle. That's right. He handed over his transportation, recreation, and self-protection. The total gift package exceeded $100,000. Why would someone do such a thing? That's what the news reporter who caught wind of the generous act inquired. "It's simple," Chas told him. "Two thousand years ago, God gave his son on the cross for our sins. So the least I can do is give him a 1969 Mustang."[1]

Speaking with Chas a couple of years after the gifts were made, I had one thing on my mind: Any regrets? Do you miss Sunday drives in the Mustang? Are you sad you'll never again reel in a largemouth bass from the deck of your MAKO? What about the rifle? Do you long for it to stand proudly in your gun safe once more?

For fifteen minutes, Chas described how things changed when he surrendered his life to Christ. And how his relationship with Jesus is now better than ever. He wanted to give his three most prized possessions to help the church, of course, but also because he didn't want anything to stand in the way of his walk with the Lord. No giver's remorse from Chas. Just giver's joy.

When did you last feel the joy of giving a costly gift?

Melissa DeGeso-Jones felt it just before Valentine's Day. She gave her husband James an unusual present. Try and guess what it was. Not a box of chocolates, tickets to a ballgame, or an evening of passionate romance. Here's a hint: James was suffering from renal failure and Melissa held the cure. Got it now? The gift weighing less than half a pound, not available through online retailers, was one healthy kidney.

Prior to the transplant surgery—before the doctor sliced Melissa open to remove her kidney and replant it into James' abdomen—she made these comments: "I'm giving as much love as I have. It's completely from my heart. James has said things to me about it being a huge sacrifice, and I said, 'It's not; it's an investment. This is our life. It's not just your life I'm giving to. There can't be an "us" without it.'"[2]

I doubt God's asking for your kidney today. But I'm certain he wants your heart.

When we give our prized possessions (like Chas), or a vital organ (like Melissa), it comes at a price. But the cost of generosity is never higher than the cost of following Christ. Eugene Peterson translates Jesus' words this way, "Simply put, if you're not willing to take what is dearest to you, whether plans or people, and kiss it goodbye, you can't be my disciple" (Luke 14:33 THE MESSAGE). No beating around the bush there.

God requires the first and best of all you have and all you are. Second place won't do. Leftovers don't cut it. Afterthoughts aren't acceptable. There's no negotiating this everlasting point. With the first commandment, the royal magistrate strikes his gavel: "You shall have no other gods before me" (Ex. 20:3). Case closed. That's why the biblical practice of tithing refers to the *first* tenth of everything God entrusts to you, not the scraps. "Honor the Lord with your wealth, with the first fruits of all your crops; then your barns will be filled to overflowing, and your vats will brim over with new wine" (Prov. 3:8-10).

And because of God's extravagant goodness toward us, the "first and best" principle goes beyond material goods to include your very being. Paul pleads, "I urge you, brothers and sisters, in view of God's mercy, to offer your bodies as a living sacrifice, holy and pleasing to God—this is your true and proper worship" (Rom. 12:1). If "living sacrifice" sounds extreme, take comfort: "There is no spiritual path more secure than that of giving yourself entirely to God."[3]

To sacrifice means to give up, yield, or surrender something precious for the sake of gaining a favored outcome. For believers, the favored outcome is living a priceless life that glorifies God and acknowledges he reigns on the highest throne. When we surrender completely and sacrifice generously, we hold nothing back from the one who gives us everything. The implication: *it's going to cost you.*

Consider the difference between a splinter in your finger and a nail through your hand. Or a pint of blood compared to all your blood. Ever been bullied at school or work? Not the same as being mocked on a cross. The God who spares no expense bids you to follow his lead. "Whoever wants to be my disciple must deny themselves and take up their cross daily and follow me" (Luke 9:23). For Abraham, God cranked up the stakes of this summons with a unique request.

A century-old man old paces the delivery room. Any moment now a promised child will enter a promised land. A year earlier, oddsmakers didn't bother to calculate the probability of this extraordinary event. You don't pluck fresh fruit off a dead tree. A dry well yields no water. Ninety-year-old women don't get pregnant. Yet on this day a son emerges from Sarah's womb and nurses at her breast. Abraham passes out cigars, news spreads around town, and an I-can't-believe-it laughter rings through the streets. But this is no joke. It all comes to pass just as God said it would. For the happy parents, Isaac was worth the wait.

Have you ever wanted something so much, for so long, the desire consumed your thoughts? And then it happens! The war ends. Peace arrives. Healing occurs. Answers appear. Your impossible dream comes true! But sometimes... without warning... it slips away like a thief in the night. The battle resumes, worries surge, pain returns, new questions arise. So much for getting your hopes up.

How does it feel when the God who fills a deep longing unexpectedly changes course? In one of the strangest stories of the Old Testament, God blesses Abraham and Sarah with a son, allows them to raise baby Isaac into boyhood, then asks Abraham to sacrifice the young man as a burnt offering on a mountain to be named later. It doesn't make sense. Isaac was a human being not a wild animal. Wasn't this test of loyalty, well... overkill?

It's surprising Abraham didn't offer God alternate options. Just a few chapters earlier he negotiated with God like a Wall Street banker when trying to save the city of Sodom. Why not barter here? *"How about my classic car, Lord, or maybe a kidney instead? Let's strike a deal. I've grown fond of this lad and I'd like to keep him around. And tell me please, how would I explain this to his mother?"* But no such conversation took place. No hint of hesitation from the father of many nations.

Authentic faith triggers eccentric behavior.

Before a drop of rain fell, Noah built an ark for a coming flood. Without a life jacket, Peter stepped off a boat to walk on a lake. Not knowing if God would save them from a king's death sentence, Shadrach, Meshach, and Abednego endured flames of a furnace rather than worship an image of gold. Faith—confidence in what one hopes for—also surrenders the outcome to God's sovereign, often mysterious, plan.

One day David slays Goliath. Another day he grieves for his slain son Absalom. One day John the Baptist baptizes Jesus. Another day Herod beheads John in prison. Before Jesus rises in glory on Sunday, he hangs in agony on Friday. Faith understands that in all things and on every day "God works for the good of those whose love him, who have been called according to his purpose" (Rom. 8:28). Even in matters of life and death.

Along with fifteen people named (and many other anonymous heroes) in the Hebrews 11 Hall of Fame, Abraham possessed the kind of faith that pierces darkness and steamrolls doubt. He modeled the proverb, "Trust in the Lord with all your heart and do not lean on your own understanding" before the words were ever written (Prov. 3:5–6 ESV). He knew the character of God and "Abraham reasoned that God could even raise the dead" (Heb. 11:19). Figuratively speaking, God did, by calling off Isaac's execution at the last possible moment. While acknowledging great relief that the ordeal ended happily, the central takeaway is Abraham passed God's test. No request from God was off-limits;

no demand out of bounds. Whatever the cost of the sacrifice, Abraham proved willing to pay it.

Contrast Abraham's response to that of a rich, young ruler looking for an expert's answer to a timeless question. In another challenging Bible story, the ruler asks Jesus, "Good teacher, what must I do to inherit eternal life?" (Luke 18:18). Jesus replies with a summary statement: Keep the commandments. After the man proudly claims to be blameless, Jesus, out of pure love, forces the confused, religious, successful man to peel back the layers of legalistic obedience and face the core of his own true nature. "You still lack one thing. Sell everything you have and give to the poor, and you will have treasure in heaven. Then come, follow me" (v. 22).

Ouch. Not expecting that. Imagine the man's eyebrows lift, then scrunch together while his face drops. The startling request collapses his world. The one thing he lacks is the main thing he needs, but the short-sighted man doesn't make the trade: earthly wealth for heavenly treasure.

What's your obstacle? The barrier standing between you and Jesus? Buckets of money or something else? Is it family or friendships or social status? Ambitious pride or stubborn rebellion? Maybe while chasing the life you think you deserve, you miss the bridge Jesus wants you to cross. What, dear friend, is the one thing *you* lack?

Don't overlook the lesson of the rich young ruler. For him, pursuing Jesus came at too high a price. But there's nothing more costly than allowing anything, anyone, anywhere, anytime, to take Jesus' place or fill his space. Honor the Lord's request. He desires to dwell in the depths of your heart. When you give up everything to follow him—a costly endeavor indeed—you open the door to a priceless life. It's a flourishing life that grasps the truth: "The will of God has nothing but sweetness, grace, and treasures for the surrendered soul."[4]

A surrendered soul, mindful of eternal realities and unconcerned about cost, searches for ways to worship the Lord. The Psalmist asks, "What can I give back to God for the blessings he's poured out on me?" (Ps. 116:12 THE MESSAGE). The answer: I'll make a toast to God. I'll praise him. I'll pray. I'll call on him. I'll do what I promised I'd do. I'll worship in God's house and sacrifice a thank offering in the presence of his people.

What else was Mary's anointing of Jesus but a sacrifice of thanksgiving, a way of showing her love? Mary was a common name in first-century Palestine, but three times the gospels mention *this* Mary, and each time she's in her usual place—at the feet of Jesus, learning, loving, serving.[5] *This* Mary witnessed her brother, Lazarus, raised from the dead. *This* Mary was listening to Jesus, absorbed by his presence, while her frazzled sister Martha focused on the hosting chores. *This* Mary was loved by Jesus: "Now Jesus loved Martha and her sister (Mary) and Lazarus" (John 11:5). And *this* Mary loved him back.

She's the one who breaks open the spikenard. The alabaster jar holds a pint of expensive perfume, worth a year's wages, and Mary doesn't hold back. Days before his death at a dinner party with friends, she empties the bottle on Jesus, pouring it out . . . out of devotion . . . out of love . . . out of gratitude . . . wiping his feet with her hair. Fragrance fills the house like the aroma of springtime orange blossoms saturating a Florida grove. Imagine the scent lifting to heaven!

Was this costly gesture really necessary? Judas thought not. Others deemed it wasteful as well. Why not sell the perfume? Use the money to feed the poor. That's more practical, right? I get it. I, too, value pragmatic frugality. At family barbecues, I've been known to ration napkins and complain about the cost of high-end paper plates. But this is different.

Judas, the thief, betrayer, and money-keeper who poisoned the minds of others, cared less about the poor than his own pocketbook. His objection had nothing to do with helping the hungry and Jesus knows it. He defends Mary and sets the record straight. And as the Anointed One predicted, centuries later we're still learning from her beautiful anointing—a preparation for burial.

Have you ever given a gift so costly your judgment was questioned? Did your uncommonly high level of generosity tilt the heads of those who know you? Was your sacrifice so extreme it drew the attention of sideline observers?

Consider the case of the Macedonians. Paul unpacks their generous deeds in two encouraging chapters written to the Corinthian Christians. He describes the situation in Macedonia this way:

> Fierce troubles came down on the people of those
> churches, pushing them to the very limit. The
> trial exposed their true colors: They were
> incredibly happy, though desperately poor. The

pressure triggered something totally unexpected:
an outpouring of pure and generous gifts. I was
there and saw it for myself. They gave offerings of
whatever they could—far more than they could
afford!—pleading for the privilege of helping out
in the relief of poor Christians.

(2 Cor. 8:2–4 THE MESSAGE)

From the world's perspective, Paul witnessed counterintuitive (some might say bizarre) behavior. Desperately poor people begging for an opportunity to share. It almost seems foolish. What prompted this sort of selfless conduct? In a word: *grace*. The Macedonians who received God's lavish grace couldn't possibly keep it to themselves. And the overflowing joy they experienced from giving far outweighed the financial cost.

Every time you give a costly gift, I pray a wave of bliss revives your soul. I hope you're motivated by the author and finisher of your faith, who, "for the joy set before him" endured the cross (Heb. 12:2). By fixing your eyes and mind and heart on things above, I trust you'll experience the beauty of God's economy.

When you value what he values, treasures await.

When you give like he gives, happiness happens.

Costly sacrifices today bring rich blessings tomorrow.

In the movie *Charlie and the Chocolate Factory*, Charlie finds the last of five golden tickets granting entrance into Willy Wonka's world-famous chocolate factory. What a glorious moment! Printed on the ticket are Mr. Wonka's promises: "Tremendous things are in store for you!" "In your wildest dreams you could not imagine the marvelous surprises that await you!"

Sounds fantastic, right? Almost like something Jesus would say.

But Charlie comes from a poor family, so after celebrating this against-all-odds find with them, he decides to sell the ticket for cash. He's already been offered five hundred bucks and knows he can get more. "We need the money more than we need the chocolate," says Charlie. He wasn't wrong. Thank goodness for Grandpa George's passionate words of blunt wisdom.

> *Young man, come here. There's plenty of money out there, they print more every day. But this ticket, there are only five of them in the whole world. And that's all there's ever going to be. Only a dummy would give this up for something as common as money. Are you a dummy?*[6]

Eyes wide as saucers, Charlie responds the only way he can: "No sir."

Now forget about gaining entrance into a chocolate factory, as delicious as that sounds. Would you give up entrance into *heaven* for something as common as money? Of course not! You're no dummy.

Digging deeper, "Would you give up something as common as money so *others* might gain entrance into heaven?

And would you give up something as common as money . . .

to feed the hungry?

shelter the homeless?

help a stranger?

cure a disease?

build a church?

support a missionary?

strengthen God's kingdom?

save a life?

express thanksgiving to God?

just for the health and happiness of it?

However costly your gift may seem, it's only money. They print more of it every day.

CHAPTER NINE

• • •

BRUSHSTROKES

How do I love thee? Let me count the ways . . .
I love thee with the breath, smiles, tears, of all my life!

ELIZABETH BARRETT BROWNING

A priest, a Levite, and a Samaritan walk into a bar.

Wait, that's not how it goes.

A priest, a Levite, and a Samaritan encounter a half-dead stranger alongside the road one day. They all ignore him. He dies.

No, that's not right either.

A priest, a Levite, and a Samaritan encounter a half-dead stranger alongside the road one day. The priest and Levite avoid him. The Samaritan drops a bag of money in the beaten man's lap and continues on his merry way.

Still not correct.

If it happened any of these ways, we wouldn't know this story.

Jesus tells a parable illustrating how to love your neighbor, reminding us that love gives. But love doesn't just give money. Love is, after all, mostly *not* about the transfer of material possessions.

The setting is a well-traveled, eighteen-mile thoroughfare descending from Jerusalem to Jericho, known for its danger and difficulty.[1] As the road ribbons through desert-like territory, its isolated stretches and rocky terrain provide ideal cover for opportunistic thieves.[2] Trading caravans and pilgrims journey together for safety. A solo traveler is a sitting duck.

The main characters—a victim, a gang of thugs, a priest, a Levite, a Samaritan, an innkeeper—play their roles.

The Victim: a little-known stranger traveling alone from Jerusalem down to Jericho.

The Gang of Thugs: your typical bad-news bandits.

The Priest: a respected clergyman with temple responsibilities. He has to remain ceremonially clean when offering sacrifices and ministering before God. Touching a dead body disqualifies him from service.

The Levite: from the tribe of Levi, an official who helps maintain the temple and its services. His sacred duties also require him to remain ceremonially clean. No dead-body contact for him, either.

The Samaritan: most Jews and Samaritans (considered halfbreeds by Jews)[3] detest one another. The intensity of their Hatfield-McCoy-like feud often erupts into violence. Few Jews wanted a Samaritan as a neighbor; they'd prefer a garbage dump next door.

The Innkeeper: witness to a remarkable medley of compassion and generosity.

As Jesus tells it, the gang of thugs rob the victim, strip him bare, pummel him to within an inch of his life, and split the scene before the cops arrive. Fortunately, a man of the cloth traveling down the same road (*away* from Jerusalem where priestly duties are performed) happens upon the half-dead man. A Spirit-led opportunity to save a life! But the priest avoids the battered man and keeps moving. The Levite, next on the scene, follows suit. The plot thickens when the Samaritan enters the picture.

Forever immortalized as the *Good* Samaritan, this foreign man comes upon the victim and doesn't keep his distance or stride past the carnage. Nor does he dial 911 to delegate the mess to paramedics. The Good Samaritan, compelled by compassion, gets personally involved. His neighborly love sparks actions—let's call them brushstrokes of generosity—which paint a portrait Jesus calls us to see.

> But a Samaritan, as he traveled, came where the
> man was; and when he saw him, he took pity on
> him. He went to him and bandaged his wounds,
> pouring on oil and wine. Then he put the man on
> his own donkey, brought him to an inn and took
> care of him. The next day he took out two denarii
> and gave them to the innkeeper. 'Look after him,'
> he said, 'and when I return, I will reimburse you
> for any extra expense you may have.'
> (Luke 10:33–35)

Brushstroke 1: He didn't ignore the victim in desperate need; he stopped to help.

Brushstroke 2: His heart went out to the stranger.

Brushstroke 3: He applied first aid and bandaged the man's wounds.

Brushstroke 4: He lifted the man onto his own donkey.

Brushstroke 5: He escorted the man to an inn and kept him comfortable.

Brushstroke 6: He stayed overnight and paid for the man's accommodations.

Brushstroke 7: He gave the innkeeper a retainer and instructions to care for the man.

Brushstroke 8: He promised to cover additional expenses.

See the big picture? His brushstrokes of generosity involved money, yes. But generosity, the manifestation of *love-that-gives*, involves so much more than financial transactions. Generosity incorporates all resources at your disposal—money, time, abilities, and going-the-extra-mile energy—as well as the palette of your emotions, especially compassion.

Jesus closes the parable with a question: "Which of these three do you think was a neighbor to the man who fell into the hands of robbers?" (Luke 10:36). Another way of wording the inquiry: "Who generously loved the stranger in need?"

We know the answer: not the religious professionals.

Pretend this parable wasn't merely a story. It's not difficult to imagine. Might we speculate about the emotional aftershocks?

Did the hardened thugs feel nothing? Just another day at the office? Or maybe one of them had a conscience stricken by guilt, shame, or remorse.

How about the priest and Levite? No need to harshly judge the holy men who likely felt bound by their duties. However, it's hard to fathom they walked away with a fountain of peace welling up inside.

The victim? Fear, pain, despair, confusion. Followed by wondrous gratitude. The kind that turns sobs of suffering into tears of joy.

And the innkeeper? Bemusement, perhaps. A front row seat to such remarkable generosity is a privilege.

Finally, the Samaritan. Because Samaritans—and all other image-bearers—possess God-given generosity genes in their DNA, perhaps he felt a great sense of satisfaction, fulfillment, and, even in the trauma of it all, happiness. Imagine a bounce in his step, cheer on his face, a glow warming his skin as he continued on his journey.

At one time or another on a different scale, maybe you've acted and felt like each of the main characters yourself: victim, thug, priest, Levite, Samaritan, innkeeper. Instead of dwelling on the past, ask yourself, "Which character do I want to be today? What emotional aftershocks do I want to feel? Could a few brushstrokes of generosity propelled by compassion and kindness grant you a *more-blessed-to-give-than-to-receive* experience? If you believe so, intentionality and creativity will be your friends.

Some years ago, a grassroots movement inspired people to practice the art of showing kindness to others—often absolute strangers. Kind people have populated the earth for centuries, but this particular movement spread like wildfire. The gestures of generosity were labeled "random acts of kindness." A foundation bearing this name formed in 1995 to celebrate and encourage participation in the refreshing enterprise. Perhaps it's more fitting to call the deeds *deliberate* acts of kindness, not *random*, because although the acts themselves might be arbitrary, for many of us kindness doesn't happen by accident. It's premeditated, calculated, intentional. A mind for kindness plans in advance, as did Trevor McKinney in the film *Pay it Forward*.

In a class assignment, Trevor shares an idea with the potential to change the planet. He wants to help three people by doing something so special it knocks their socks off. Instead of paying it back, he hopes each recipient pays the favor forward to three more people that same day. And the day after, nine beneficiaries repeat the pattern. And so on, until an epidemic of benevolence ensues. If you do the multiplication, two short weeks later nearly five million people would be blessed by the outbreak of kindness.

"Well Trevor, the class seems to think you've come up with an overly utopian idea," says the teacher.[4] Perhaps they are right, but that doesn't stop Trevor. Nor should it stop you.

How many ways can you show kindness and love? How many ways can you express generosity? How might you launch an epidemic? Hold that thought.

During her courtship with Robert Browning in 1846, Elizabeth Barrett penned *Sonnet 43, "How Do I Love Thee?"* The poem articulated the consuming devotion she felt for her future husband. Her word choices—"depth," "breadth," "height," "freely," "purely," "passion," and "soul"—make an indelible impression on the reader. Elizabeth's iconic poem was far more refined than the love note I passed to a girl named Anne in first grade: *I love you. Will you be my Valentine? XXX. OOO. P.S.—Did you know I can spell hippopotamus?*

The line following "How do I love thee?" opens a thousand doors: "Let me count the ways." Better yet, let me *begin* to count the ways because they're innumerable. A fourteen-line sonnet merely gets things rolling. To fully describe love it would take more words than the Library of Congress contains. And a slight modification of the question, "How *do* I love thee?" to "How *can*

I love thee?" or "How can I *show* you love?" surfaces a parallel universe of possibilities. No end exists to the variety of ways to generously express genuine love.

How might your diverse expressions—your own brushstrokes of generosity—transform lives? Would they make the world a better place? Could one brushstroke feed a hungry mouth? And another lift a lonely heart? Might a brushstroke restore a suffering saint to physical, emotional, or spiritual health? Or lead a sinner to Christ? Best-selling author Thomas Cahill notes the effect of prioritizing generous acts:

> If Christians had put kindness ahead of devotion
> to good order, theological correctness, and our
> own justifications—if we had followed in the
> footsteps of the heretical Samaritan who was
> willing to wash someone else's wounds rather than
> the self-regarding steps of the priest and the
> immaculate steps of the Levite—the world we
> inhabit would be a very different one.[5]

Indeed, the world would be a better place. And what about you? How would these actions transform your own life? Can you imagine your level of happiness rise, your health and well-being surge, your sense of purpose swell like a tidal wave? "A generous person will prosper; whoever refreshes others will be refreshed" (Prov. 11:25). That's a win-win.

To that noble end, let's unpack a few ways to decorate the world's canvas with brushstrokes of generosity, beginning with the most obvious.

BE GENEROUS WITH YOUR
MONEY AND MATERIAL POSSESSIONS

Even as we emphasize money isn't the only way to convey generosity, we cannot skip this category. The Bible doesn't; nor does Jesus. For some needs, cash is the suitable cure. Plus, how we use our tangible goods reveals the content of our hearts and state of our faith.

John, the disciple whom Jesus loved, wonders, "If anyone has material possessions and sees a brother or sister in need but has no pity on them, how can the love of God be in that person?" (1 John 3:17). Jesus' younger half-brother, James, says your faith is hollow if you neglect fellow believers who need clothing or food. "If one of you says to them, 'Go in peace; keep warm and well fed,' but does nothing about their physical needs, what good is it?" (James 2:16).

The devoted disciples in the early church modeled financial generosity. "And they were selling their possessions and belongings and distributing the proceeds to all, as any had need" (Acts 2:45 ESV). This close-knit community ate together, prayed together, lived together, and loved each other with glad and sincere hearts. Every day a celebration. No wonder "the Lord added to their number daily those who were being saved" (v. 47). Brushstrokes of generosity draw a crowd.

Look carefully in the Bible and notice as money changes hands and properties are retitled. The instances range from obligatory tithing by the Pharisees to the sacrificial gift of the widow's mite.

Zacchaeus the taxman morphed from a collector of money

into a giver of money. After a treetop encounter with Jesus, he promised half his wealth to the poor and a fourfold payback to anyone he'd cheated.[6] Now, that's a conversion.

Joseph of Arimathea donated his new tomb. He wrapped Jesus' crucified body in clean linens and buried him there.[7] A grave for God. That kind of giving opportunity doesn't come around every day! Of course, our Lord only borrowed the space for three days, so does it really count? Let's be generous and give him credit anyway.

Another Joseph, a Levite from Cyprus, sold a field and plopped the proceeds at the apostles' feet for distribution to the needy.[8] Perhaps that's one reason why the apostles renamed the guy Barnabas, which means Son of Encouragement.

Then recall the boy who handed over his Happy Meal (five barley loaves and two small fish) to feed five thousand men and their accompanying families.[9] How's that for making lunch go a long way?

One of my favorite giving stories involves an aged King David at an ancient fundraising dinner. To build a permanent temple for worshiping God, he gathered a stack of materials and pile of precious metals. But in his devotion he also forked over his personal treasure of silver and gold. All of it. His announced brushstroke of generosity sparked an inspired response. Other leaders jumped in. They did swan dives and cannonballs into the deep end of the giving pool. The assembly of people "rejoiced at the willing response of their leaders, for they had given freely and wholeheartedly to the Lord" (1 Chron. 29:9).

After the giving frenzy King David prays. His benediction

articulates profound realities of the grandest scale. The words move me like few other paragraphs in the Bible. To my ears, a summary of 1 Chronicles 29:10–19 sounds like this:

> *Praise be to you, O Lord, God, our Father. Yours is the greatness and power and glory and majesty and splendor and strength. It's your kingdom. You're the creator. You're the ruler. You're the owner. We know you're the One who gives us wealth and honor and strength. So . . . Thank you, Lord. We praise your glorious name. How can it even be said that we're giving generously? Everything in our hands came from you! It's all yours, anyway. Isn't that obvious?*
>
> *This world isn't our home and this life is like a shadow. Here today, gone tomorrow. So, I gave willingly with pure motives and these people joined me. What a joyful experience! Now, here's my prayer: keep this spirit of generosity alive in the hearts of your people forever. And keep our hearts loyal to you.*

The king concludes with this edict: "Praise the Lord your God" (1 Chron. 29:20). And praise him, they did.

Is it possible, 3,000 years later, David's prayer still echoes in the chambers of God's heart? Why wouldn't it? Prayers don't evaporate. Prayers don't decay. Prayers don't get lost in a pile of paperwork. Prayers don't get filed and forgotten. And unlike the perishables in your refrigerator, prayers don't have expiration dates. Maybe your own brushstrokes of generosity are a residual by-product of David's request: "Keep this spirit of generosity alive in the hearts of your people forever." If you get to heaven before me, tell David we're grateful he prayed for us.

No substitute for financial generosity exists. But generosity doesn't end there. When you tuck away your wallet, hang on to your paintbrush. Add more brushstrokes to the portrait you're creating. Watch the scene blossom into a finished work of art.

BE GENEROUS WITH YOUR TIME

I know ... you're busy. I'm busy. Everyone's busy. Hungry to get ahead, we hustle. Driven to succeed, we scurry. Anxious to accumulate assets, we grind. Preoccupied with status, we strive. Days fly by amid a hurricane of activity. We remain overcommitted, overscheduled, overloaded, and overstressed. No rest for the weary parent. No margin for the working warrior. Locating an open slot on your calendar is as easy as finding a four-leaf clover in a frozen desert.

You have people to meet, places to go, things that-won't-matter-a-thousand-years-from-now to do. Responsibilities. Engage-ments. Appointments. Commitments. Pages of life filled with trivial pursuits. Oh sure, some of it is important, productive, and absolutely necessary, but as legendary UCLA basketball coach John Wooden put it, "Never mistake activity for achievement." If all your plate-spinning feels like nothing but a circus act, put down the dishes and pay attention for a moment.

When tyranny of the urgent makes time your scarcest

resource... your most valuable commodity... the hardest thing to give away... remember time is precious, yes. But people... people are *more* precious. People matter more than spinning plates. Or anything.

Would you like to fluster less and flourish more? Want your songs to exceed your sighs?[10] Care to reduce exasperation and increase jubilation? Then make sure your inputs produce worthwhile outputs. Use your limited time to practice limitless generosity.

Your brushstrokes might take fractions of a second, like when you smile at a stranger, wink at a baby, nod your approval, and—when you're running late in rush hour traffic—allow the silver-haired lady with a blinking turn signal to merge into your congested lane.

Or your generous acts could take a minute or two, as does our nightly routine. Before bedtime, I close the window blinds so Mary Ann feels safe. She loads the coffeemaker so it's ready for the morning (this isn't a one-cup Keurig). Some years ago, I mentioned it meant a lot to me when she did the coffee prep work, because I hate to cook. Now, when I wake up and press the brewing machine's start button, gurgling noises begin, I smell coffee, and I remember my wife loves me. While the pot fills black, I open the blinds and prove I love her, too.

Occasionally, your time-gift takes longer, even a full lifespan, such as when you commit to the calling of vocational ministry. Even if you don't abandon fishing nets to become a full-time apostle or leave your homeland to serve as a foreign missionary or surrender your best years to aid the poor in Calcutta's slums, you're still called to a lifetime of service. The "good works" you were created for (Eph. 2:10); the instruction to "look not only to your own interests, but also the interests of others" (Phil. 2:4); the command to "do good to everyone" (Gal. 6:10); "show hospitality" (Rom. 12:13); "serve one another humbly in love" (Gal. 5:13); "carry each other's burdens" (Gal. 6:2); "spur one another on toward love" (Heb. 10:24); "look after orphans and widows" (James 1:27); "live in harmony" (Rom. 12:16); "comfort one another" (2 Cor. 13:11); and the catchall, "offer your bodies as a living sacrifice" (Rom. 12:1) will cost you time.

Be generous with your seconds, minutes, hours, and days. And don't grow weary of doing good, because "at just the right time we will reap a harvest of blessing if we don't give up" (Gal. 6:9 NLT).

Make a colorful mark on the world. Notice needs. Volunteer. Offer to help. Do a five-minute favor of any flavor, for somebody . . . anybody.[11] Read a book to a child. Speak words of encouragement. Say something uplifting. Write a note. Mail a card. Send a text. Listen, really listen. Mind your manners. Mentor someone. Laugh at a dad joke. Babysit for free. Invite someone home for dinner. Bring a meal to a family in need. Host a block party. Pet your dog. Pet a stray cat, but wear gloves while you do it. Care for your friend's pet while they're on vacation.

You can do the laundry or mow the lawn, especially when it's not your assigned task. Hold open a door. Pick up garbage. Pray for others. Keep praying. Forgive others. Forgive yourself. Keep forgiving. Donate blood. Give someone a ride. Stop and pick up donuts on your way into the office. Visit your grandma. Visit the sick. Visit those in prison. If your grandma is sick in prison, visit her today. And please, let that silver-haired lady with the blinking turn signal merge into your lane already. It might be your grandma breaking out of jail.

BE GENEROUS WITH YOUR TALENTS, ABILITIES, AND GIFTS

There's a nuanced distinction between natural talents, special abilities, and spiritual gifts, but for simplicity's sake let's lump them together. Like a birthmark, these distinguishing characteristics make you, you. And you're one of a kind. Heaven houses no assembly line to produce humans. Fingerprints and retinal scans prove each blueprint is used just once. That's why it's critical to never downplay your skills or neglect your duty to deploy them. Without your unique brushstrokes, something's missing in the world.

You may not write like Shakespeare or speak like Churchill. You can't preach like Billy Graham or pray like Mother Teresa. Few can rhyme like Dr. Seuss or run like Usain Bolt. Not many brains function like Einstein's and not many arms throw a baseball like Nolan Ryan's. No matter. *Your* talents, abilities, and gifts are a big deal. God endowed you with the exact strength and blend of skills he wants you to have, and he's not comparing your potential with what others are able to do.

That's why your fingerpainting hangs on God's refrigerator right next to the Mona Lisa. God simply desires that you use what he's given you—whatever the results—for his glory. He wants your light to shine before others, "that they may see your good deeds and glorify your Father in heaven" (Matt. 5:16).

Invest your unique talents in the kingdom, don't bury them

in the dirt. As John Piper pleads, "Don't waste your life."

> If you want your life to count, if you want the
> ripple effect of the pebbles you drop to become
> waves that reach the ends of the earth and roll on
> for centuries and eternity, you don't have to have a
> high IQ or a high EQ. You don't have to have good
> looks or riches. You don't have to come from a fine
> family or a fine school. You just have to know a few
> great, majestic, unchanging, obvious, simple,
> glorious things, and be set on fire by them.[12]

One of the glorious things to know is, "For we are God's handiwork, created in Christ Jesus to do good works, which God prepared in advance for us to do" (Eph. 2:10). If you were searching for your purpose, congratulations! Look no further.

Find your sweet spot to serve. Slip into your unique groove. Develop your gifts and utilize your strengths.

What do you have a flair for?

Where do you excel?

What draws your interest and piques your curiosity?

Where do your experience, education, and passion intersect?

What brings you joy?

Trial and error will teach you. Friends and family will encourage you when you're on the right track and warn you when you're not. Singing solos onstage isn't everyone's bag.

BE GENEROUS TO YOUR SPOUSE, FAMILY, FRIENDS, THE NEEDY, AND THOSE WHO SEEMINGLY DON'T DESERVE IT

Don't leave anyone out when choosing where to direct your generosity—including yourself. After all, how will you ever love your enemies if you don't treat yourself with compassion and kindness? Sometimes you need to give yourself a break. God does.

In any encounter with another human, ask yourself, "How can I serve this person?"[13]

What act would help this widow? What can I do for this orphan? How can I assist this stranger? How might I love my archrival? Would a kind word, large check, friendly smile, or handwritten note serve them best?

In your quest to be inclusive, be careful not to overlook those you love the deepest. In all our busyness, we're prone to take our closest friends, family, and even spouse for granted. I left a hand-written list of tasks for myself sitting on the table one day and darted off to work. When I returned home, I noticed an extra bullet point at the bottom of the page: *Hug your wife and give her more attention.* Message received.

Find opportunities to freely give your time, talent, and treasure. Don't overlook anyone. Stranger, spouse, self. Friend, foreigner, foe. Think of it: God-inspired, DNA-wired generosity offered to everyone. As Paul wrote to the Galatian Christians, "Therefore, as we have opportunity, let us do good to all people, especially to those who belong to the family of believers" (Gal. 6:10). And "The King will reply, 'Truly I tell you, whatever you did for the least of these brothers and sisters of mine, you did for me'" (Matt. 25:40).

Be a generosity artist. The world can't wait for your priceless brushstrokes.

CHAPTER TEN

◆ ◆ ◆

PRICELESS

All truths are easy to understand once they are discovered;
the point is to discover them.

GALILEO GALILEI (1564–1642)

*T*he guy had brains.

He was an inventor, philosopher, astronomer, and math geek. He engineered ancient weapons of war, pioneered the field of physics, and designed a class of navy ships. He discovered the secrets of geometry, harnessed the power of pulleys and levers, and moved streams of water with a spinning screw. Some call Archimedes one of the greatest scientists ever, on par with Newton, Einstein, Euclid, and the genius who invented glazed doughnuts. It's surprising the story he's most well known for finds him sprinting down the street, stark naked, yelling at the top of his lungs.

What amazing breakthrough triggered the streaking incident? It involved a shady craftsman, a king, a gold crown, and a bathtub. Through water displacement, Archimedes figured out a way to identify metals via their mass and found a royal crown, purportedly made of solid gold, wasn't as pure as its maker claimed. Moments after his sudden discovery the giddy scientist lost his mind. He dashed down the block in his birthday suit, shouting the words he's famous for: *Eureka, I have found it!*

Have you ever experienced a eureka moment? A sudden flash of insight or golden revelation? I have. I'll share it with you—but no streaking, please. Here's my epiphany: *The happiest people I know are the most generous people I know, and the most generous people I know are the happiest people I know.* Not mind-blowing at first, perhaps, but give it time to bloom. Once the truth takes root, it may grow like a spring tulip in the garden of your soul.

Generous people are generally happy. They experience an "it's more blessed to give than to receive" existence because they've learned the timeless truths we've been talking about that foster a priceless life.

So, what is a priceless life?

It's the life our Savior lived for you and the one he wants you to experience today. Our adversary advances a different mission. Jesus says, "The thief comes only to steal and kill and destroy. I came that they may have life and have it abundantly" (John 10:10 ESV). Note the black and white contrast here. It strikes like a ninja. Satan comes *only* to wreak havoc. *All* of his candy-coated lies are meant to tempt, trip, distract, and damage us. Destruction awaits those who are deceived by his wiles. Jesus, however, comes to give life.

Life . . . abundant life . . . a priceless life . . . for *you*!

In 1997, Mastercard introduced an ingenious advertising campaign. Its purpose was to "showcase enduring moments in life and shine a light on what is truly priceless."[1] The first television commercial in the series featured a father-son outing to a major league baseball game. Camera shots show them enter the stadium. They visit the concession stand. They locate their seats as the action starts. This has all the makings of a day to remember. In a gentle monotone with a mellow music underscore, a narrator describes the scene:

Two tickets: $28.

Two hot dogs, two popcorns, and two sodas: $18.

One autographed baseball: $45.

Real conversation with 11-year-old son: Priceless.

There are some things money can't buy. For everything else there's Mastercard.

Priceless experiences are everywhere. Sometimes they are anticipated, occurring on milestone days when a child is born or a couple in love declares, "I do." But priceless moments catch you by surprise, too. Like when that child takes her first steps or the couple in love—fifty years later, bodies worn down and souls braided together—share a front-porch, rocking-chair conversation recounting decades of serendipitous blessings. Sweet memories linger, rich joys to recall.

However, the *best* things money can't buy come from Jesus. In the truest sense of the word, what Jesus did for you is priceless.

- *He departed the glories of heaven for you.* "But he gave up his place with God and made himself nothing. He was born as a man and became like a servant" (Phil. 2:7 NCV).

- *He abandoned riches for you.* "For you know the grace of our Lord Jesus Christ, that though he was rich, yet for your sakes he became poor, so that you through his poverty might become rich" (2 Cor. 8:9).

- *He brought you to God.* "For Christ also suffered once for sins, the righteous for the unrighteous, to bring you to God . . ." (1 Pet. 3:18).

- *He grants you freedom.* "You, my brothers and sisters, were called to be free" (Gal. 5:13). "It is for freedom that Christ has set us free" (Gal. 5:1).

- *He offers you rest.* "Come to me, all you who are weary and burdened, and I will give you rest" (Matt. 11:28).

- *He left you his peace.* "Peace I leave with you; my peace I give you. I do not give to you as the world gives. Do not let your hearts be troubled and do not be afraid" (John 14:27).

- *He loves you to death.* "But God demonstrates his own love for us in this: While we were still sinners, Christ died for us" (Rom. 5:8).

- *He conquered the grave for you.* "Where, O death is your victory? Where, O death is your sting?" (1 Cor. 15:55).

- *He made you righteous.* "God made him who had no sin to be sin for us, so that in him we might become the righteousness of God" (2 Cor. 5:21).

- *He is preparing a place for you.* "My Father's house has many rooms; if that were not so, would I have told you that I am going there to prepare a place for you?" (John 14:2).

- *He is coming back for you.* "And if I go and prepare a place for you, I will come back and take you to be with me that you also may be where I am" (John 14:3).

In human terms, Jesus left the peaks of the Pyrenees for Death Valley. He gave up Fort Knox for an empty wallet. Built a bridge to God over a black abyss. Defeated the dragon of death with a decisive blow. He won the battle of all ages, then took a key forged from his risen body and unlocked the front door of your penitentiary. And the future home he's preparing for you? Well, let's just say neither Martha Stewart nor the entire Magnolia Network could make it any cozier. The Chief Architect has a flair for design.

How generous of Jesus to do all this . . . and more . . . for *you*.

Jesus makes daring claims in John's gospel, calling himself the bread of life, light of the world, and gate for the sheep. He's the good shepherd, the resurrection and the life, and the way and the truth and the life. (See how the word *life* keeps popping up?) In his seventh "I AM" statement, he's the true vine that yes, connects us to life. Through these intriguing aliases, he grants us a richer, deeper way to understand what he offers.

And still, we could add pages to this catalog of generosity. "His mercies never come to an end; they are new every morning . . ." (Lam. 3:22–23 ESV). The only fair way to complete a list of Jesus' generous acts is by repeating the statement John made when he tied a bow around his good news digest: "Jesus did many other things as well. If every one of them were written down, I suppose that even the whole world would not have room for the books that would be written" (John 21:25).

How to put a price tag on that? Impossible.

What Jesus did (and is still doing) for you and me is priceless. It matters not whether we feel worthy enough to deserve his benevolence (we're not)—his view of us won't veer. To him, you and I are priceless. Puncture the balloon of inferior thoughts and slam the door on doubt. Yes, our sins are dirty. But as we walk in the light, "the blood of Jesus, his son, purifies us from all sin (1 John 1:7). Yes, we've failed. However, we'll never fail to be loved by the Lord. With the strongest words imaginable, Paul announces not just how great God's love is for us, but also how sticky it is. No force in the known or unknown universe can separate us from his affection.

> For I am convinced that neither death nor life,
> neither angels nor demons, neither the present
> nor the future, nor any powers, neither height nor
> depth, nor anything else in all creation, will be
> able to separate us from the love of God that is in
> Christ Jesus our Lord.
>
> (Rom. 8:38–39)

Personally, I take great comfort knowing God's love orbits every atom in my body like swirling electrons. But I'm acutely aware of the truth that I am not the only one he loves. Not the only person marked with a "priceless" price tag. Not the only soul he died for. God gave . . . because he so loved the *world*. This includes people who don't look like me, think like me, or act like me. They don't speak like me, dress like me, or vote like me. They might even root for a rival sports team that trampled my beloved franchise in the playoffs.

Put it together—the priceless life of Jesus and the fact that we are all priceless to him—and you discover the secret to living a priceless life. *Live* like Jesus. *Give* like Jesus. Lavishly, cheerfully, graciously, and gratefully. With everything you've got.

I love putting together jigsaw puzzles. The activity is a form of mental yoga, and it feels like I'm accomplishing something. One of my favorite brands claims their product was made in the land of love. Another comes with a happiness guarantee.[2] The maker promises when you flip over, sort, frame, and assemble 1,000 miniature pieces of cardboard, you'll be delighted with the puzzle experience as well as the finished product. Aren't generous acts similar? They come from a place where love resides, happiness ensues, and an image of beauty is shaped.

Generous people experience the jigsaw puzzle phenomenon because they embrace the paradox of Jesus' words: "It is more blessed to give than to receive" (Acts 20:35). At first glance, the statement might sound like a government agent who claims, "I'm from the IRS and I'm here to help," or a dentist who promises, "This won't hurt a bit." But this isn't a trap. It's the truth. Jesus doesn't work for Uncle Sam and he isn't trying to pull your teeth. The revelation—you're far happier giving than getting—is merely a spiritual paradox, not unlike others Jesus shares that flip our world upside down. Check these out from Matthew's gospel:

- "Whoever wants to be great among you must be your servant." (Matt. 20:26)

- "So the last will be first, and the first will be last." (Matt. 20:16)

- "For those who exalt themselves will be humbled, and those who humble themselves will be exalted." (Matt. 23:12)

- "Whoever finds their life will lose it, and whoever loses their life for my sake will find it." (Matt. 10:39)

Alongside these paradoxes are hundreds of biblical "*so that*" statements[3] which explain the reason *for* or result *of* a particular situation or action. A few questions and answers to consider:

Q: Why does God help you stand steady and strong?

A: "He will also keep you firm to the end, *so that* you will be blameless on the day of our Lord Jesus Christ" (1 Cor. 1:8).

Q: Why does God embrace us with compassion in times of need?

A: "[He] comforts us in all our troubles, *so that* we can comfort those in any trouble with the comfort we ourselves receive from God" (2 Cor. 1:4).

Q: Why does God bless you beyond what anyone deserves?

A: "And God is able to bless you abundantly, *so that* in all things at all times, having all that you need, you will abound in every good work" (2 Cor. 9:8).

Q: And finally, why does God give you the ability to (among other things) earn income and accumulate wealth?

A: "You will be made rich in every way *so that* you can be

generous on every occasion, and through us your generosity will result in thanksgiving to God" (2 Cor. 9:11).

Let that last verse settle.

This is something I'm still learning. Confession time. During the past months I've worked on this book, you know, trying to assemble and organize a few helpful and encouraging words about generosity, Mary Ann has occasionally looked at me and asked, "Uh... do you really think you should be writing this book?" Emphasis on the word you. What? Ouch!

She asked me when I didn't want to pick up the dinner tab at the restaurant with our adult kids. (They make more money than us, and I've already spent a few bucks raising them.)

She asked me when I hesitated to lend our horse trailer to a neighbor. (I had just repaired it, it's thirty years old and finicky, and I'm too busy to work on it if something breaks.)

She asked me when I complained about babysitting three of our grandsons for an entire weekend. (As much as I love them, I didn't have the energy for forty-eight straight hours of nonstop boys. And I really wanted to play golf that Saturday.)

Those weren't the only times she asked me, but I'm reluctant to reveal the more embarrassing instances.

I know her intentions. I know her heart. And I'm happy she confronted me. She was honestly trying to help and I'm a better person because of it. I also know my litany of lame rationalizations wouldn't hold up in the King's court.

What do I do when I feel unable, unwilling, or unmotivated to be generous? When my hands are clenched instead of open?

When I'm hanging on instead of handing out? When I'm struggling to share money, possessions, time, abilities, and energy with others? How do I reset my giving perspective when complications of life overwhelm me, busyness distracts me, a scarcity mentality infects me, and self-absorbed "but-I-work-hard-for-my-money" thoughts pollute my mind like a river of toxic waste?

Glad you asked. Perhaps, on occasion, you wrestle with similar beasts.

First, I realize I'm still growing in my faith, learning to trust my provider. By no means did I grow up in poverty, but as a family of seven living on a meatcutter's wages, money was always tight. When I wanted to play little league baseball, the eight-dollar sign-up fee was nearly a deal-breaker. I'll never forget my father's interrogation: "Are you sure you want to play, Michael? Eight dollars is a lot of money!"

I ended up playing mostly rightfield for the Robins that season, but the eight-dollar lecture haunts me to this day. You might say it was an expensive conversation. Similar childhood experiences shaped my early views of spending, saving, and giving— views God's word is still reforming in me today.

Second, I resolve to live the life of purpose and meaning to which I've been called. And since there's no upper limit on how much I'm to love God and my neighbor, by default, I'm called to be generous. George Bernard Shaw's words inspire me onward:

> I want to be used for a purpose recognized by
> myself as a mighty one; be thoroughly worn out
> before I am thrown on the scrap heap; be a force

of nature rather than a feverish, selfish little clod
of ailments and grievances complaining that the
world will not devote itself to making me happy.

Third, I recall occasions when people have been generous to me and instances when I've been generous to others. I can't help but smile as a rainforest of refreshment washes over me. Breathing slows and my stress level sinks. Worries fade and my sense of well-being rises. You can try this exercise at home, it's not dangerous.

Finally, I remember the timeless truths we've covered in this book. We serve a happy God. He's the Great Giver, Life-Giver, and Generous One. We're crafted in his image, born and wired to give. Everything we need, we can trust God has for us. Life is about loving people, not possessions or positions. Contentment and gratitude safeguard us from the black hole of materialism. Giving can be costly, but it's always worth the price. And generosity is about more than money—it's about everything—because there are a zillion ways to love someone.

What do people want most out of life? Good health, fulfillment, and a sense of security. A loving family, close friends, and personal freedom. Opportunity, meaningful work, and a lasting legacy.[4] But of all the common desires, one rises above the rest: most of all . . . people want to be happy. "There is no one who does not wish to be happy."[5] And as we've discovered, generous people are happy people.

May you get what you want out of your beautiful life. May you find more happiness than you ever dreamed possible. May you feel grateful and privileged to call yourself blessed. May you sense the radiant wonder of God's glorious love. And may you, in the spirit of generosity, share with others the precious secret to living a priceless life.

QUESTIONS

• • •

FOR REFLECTION

QUESTIONS

FOR REFLECTION

CHAPTER ONE QUESTIONS
THE GREAT GIVER

Look Back

1. God displays the *breadth* of his affection in ways we often overlook. Because nothing is impossible for the King of kings and Lord of lords, the manifestations of his generosity are endless.

   - Why do we so often overlook God's affectionate actions? What are some ways he's shown love to you?
   - What are some specific examples of God's diverse and abundant generosity? Consider everything from the wonders of nature to human relationships and emotions.
   - How would life change if you faithfully prayed: "Show me, Lord, how you're being generous to me today"?

2. He is, after all, the Great Giver. The Life Giver. The Generous One. And we should note at this point and never forget it: No being is happier than God.

   - Do you often think of God as being happy? How do you usually picture God's emotional state? Euphorically happy? Frequently disappointed? Frustrated or angry? Or something else? Is he smiling or frowning at this very moment?
   - How is your happiness similar to and different from God's happiness?

3. God didn't create the heavens and earth on a whim. Purpose inspired design. Father, Son, and Spirit made a world where everything was good, for us to enjoy.

- List some things in creation that you enjoy.
- What natural wonders have you seen that struck you with a sense of awe?
- When you revisit these experiences, does it still invoke a sense of appreciation and amazement?

4. Generosity is at its essence a measurement of abundance. Generosity equals a spirit of unselfishness multiplied by quantity: $G = u * q$. It's giving anything—talent, time, treasure (and more)—freely, abundantly, wholeheartedly, happily, for the good and well-being of another.

- How would you add to or change this definition of generosity?
- When it comes to acting generously, how important is motive?
- Can you identify generosity when you see it?

5. Jesus was with you yesterday, he's with you today, and he'll be with you tomorrow. You might say Jesus is generous with his time. And he wants to spend it with people like you.

- Do you really think Jesus wants to spend time with you? Why or why not?
- Consider the plight of the people Jesus befriended, healed, and otherwise interacted with. Can you identify with any of their stories? Explain.
- If Jesus lived next door, do you think he'd invite you over for dinner? Would you return the favor?

6. "When Jacob awoke from his sleep he thought, 'Surely the Lord is in this place and I was not aware of it'" (Genesis 28:16).

- How did Jacob respond to the sudden realization of God's immediate presence?
- Describe a time when you suddenly realized the Lord was present. How did you respond? With amazement, fear, unworthiness, or something else? Did you consider it a sacred moment?

7. When you were shipwrecked, marooned on a giant block of floating ice, tossed by winds and waves, distant from the priceless life you were born to live—cold, wet, hungry, hopeless, and helpless—Jesus came to save you.
   - Describe what was happening in your life when Jesus found you.
   - Who was happier when you accepted his offer of grace: you or Jesus?
   - Do you really believe that angels rejoiced when you were rescued from your shipwrecked life?

8. Why did you decide to read *Happily Generous*? What do you hope to gain from this book? What does it mean to live a priceless life?

Look Up

1. Read Exodus 13:21–22; 16:11–18; 17:8–16; 20:1–17; and Deuteronomy 29:5.
   - How did God provide for the Israelites as they wandered in the wilderness? Why did God do the things he did?
   - To care for his people, God is generous with his power, presence, and provision. Which of these Godly expressions of love do you need most in your life today?

2. Meditate on Psalm 103:2–5.

  ◆ Name some God-provided benefits the Psalmist encourages
    us to remember. Which of his benefits stand out to you the
    most at this stage in your life?

  ◆ Why do you think the writer opens and closes Psalm 103
    with the words, "Praise the Lord, my soul"?

CHAPTER TWO QUESTIONS
BORN FOR THIS

Look Back

1. Who are you? Where did you come from? Where are you going? And what are you here to do?
   - Do you ever feel like a modernday Sisyphus, trapped in a cycle of unfulfilling routines?
   - What happens when a person derives their values, purpose, and meaning from worldly sources—including social media, celebrity influencers, Wall Street, and Main Street, U.S.A.?
   - How would you describe your true identity?
   - How often do you reflect on the divine purpose of your life? From where is your purpose derived?

2. Although your birth and death certificates might cite dates spanning eighty-plus years, as you age those years zoom by faster and scrunch closer together.
   - Has it been your experience that as you age time speeds up? Why do you think this is the case? What can you do to slow time down?
   - Does an awareness of life's brevity create urgency in how you prioritize daily activities? Does it make you think twice about "wishing away" time?
   - Are you in the habit of living in the past? The future? When do you most feel like you're living in the present?

3. The Teacher's firsthand experience with worldly exploits left him hollow and unsatisfied.

- Which of the following pursuits can end up feeling meaningless? Why?
  - Wisdom, knowledge, and understanding.
  - Pleasure and laughter.
  - Work projects.
  - Acquiring possessions.
- Why do people look for meaning in so many ways and places? In what ways have you searched for significance? Were you successful?
- What is the Teacher's ultimate conclusion (Ecclesiastes 12:13)?

4. Theologian Michael Eaton writes, "The preacher (teacher) wishes to drive us to see that God is there, that he is good and generous, and that only such an outlook makes life coherent and fulfilling."
   - Do you agree with this insight? Why or why not?
   - What makes life coherent and fulfilling for you?

5. The Westminster Shorter Catechism asks, "What is the chief end of man?" and answers, *"Man's chief end is to glorify God and enjoy him forever."*
   - What does that statement mean to you? Is this an accurate summary of your understanding of mankind's purpose?
   - How does generosity fit into this picture?

6. If you accept the premise that God is the Great Giver and you're crafted in his image, you'll realize generosity resides in your DNA.

- Do you agree your calling and purpose—to bless others generously—is wrapped in your identity as a child of God?
- What can happen when we let our light shine before others?
- When Paul encourages generosity, he connects the behavior with an outcome described as "life that is truly life." Do you have firsthand knowledge of this reality?

7. When Jesus knew the time had come for him to leave this world, there were different ways he could have spent his final hours. Among other options, he could have decided to extend his stay, deliver a lecture, demand a tribute, develop an evangelism strategy, decipher a mystery, or destroy an enemy.
   - What did he do and why? Do his actions surprise you? Why or why not? How do his actions fulfill his life's purpose? What did he say would happen to those who followed his example?
   - Imagine you're a news reporter live on camera at the Last Supper. Jesus begins washing his disciple's feet. How do you describe the scene to viewers at home? Which disciple would you interview first? What would you ask Peter? Judas? Jesus?
   - If you knew you had twenty-four hours left to live, what would you do and why?

Look Up

1. Read Matthew 22:37–40. Fill in the blank: The first and greatest commandment is to love _____ and the second is to love _____.

- With what faculties are you to love God?
- How are you to love people? Why does Jesus say it this way?
- In both instances, does it sound as if Jesus is saying to love *generously*?

2. Read Matthew 28:18–20. What were Jesus' final instructions to his eleven remaining disciples?

- Do you believe those words are still applicable for us today?
- How is the Great Commission connected to the Great Commandment?
- How will a generous spirit help us live according to our calling?

CHAPTER THREE QUESTIONS
WHAT HOLDS YOU BACK?

Look Back

1. Sometimes generosity is complicated. Invitations to give come your way and you want to be generous but not crazy. You're willing to sacrifice but not suffer. You listen to the Spirit but your flesh whispers, too: *Let's not go overboard.*
   - How do you relate to the complicated nature of generosity?
   - Are you ever convicted or conflicted when asked to give? Cite an example.

2. Only thirteen percent of evangelicals tithe, and historically, followers of Jesus give in a range of two to three percent of what they earn. Half of evangelical Protestants contribute less than one percent of their total income to church and charity. Many Christians give absolutely nothing.
   - Do these giving statistics surprise you? Why or why not?
   - Can you be an authentic follower of Jesus and never give financially? Explain your answer.

3. You're reading this book to move forward in your generosity journey, not sink into emotional quicksand. Self-deprecating feelings won't help.
   - When it comes to giving, do you ever feel guilt, pride, or ambivalence? Are these emotions helpful or hurtful? How so?
   - Most people say they'd like to be more generous than they already are. Do you feel that way too, or are you satisfied

with your current level of generosity? What are your reasons for not giving more?

- In Romans 7, the apostle Paul describes the tension between his spiritual desires and ability to live them out. Do you ever feel this tension? Does it confuse you? How do you deal with this common human experience?

4. When the fear of not having enough inhibits our generosity, we hold on, pull back, cling to, and stockpile.

- How does a scarcity mentality affect the way you spend, save, live, and give?

- Did you grow up in a household of abundance or scarcity? If you had siblings or a blended family, did you ever compete for limited resources? How did that feel?

- How do you think your early childhood experiences affect your attitude toward generosity today?

5. A proper assessment of our personal resources is essential.

- Do you have more time or less time than the average person in your community? Explain your answer.

- Consider your talents, gifts, and abilities. Are you happy with what God has endowed you with? Can you see how your unique composition and capacities can be useful in God's kingdom?

- Consider your financial situation. How does your income and net asset level compare with others? Keep in mind, ninety-five percent of the world's population earn less than $30,000 annually and more than fifty percent of all adults have less than $10,000 in total assets.

◆ Does a review of your current resources (time, talent, and treasure) make you think you have more to give or less to give? As you manage the resources God has entrusted to you, can you identify any adjustments you want to make?

Look Up

1. Read John 10:9–11. Based on this passage, why did Jesus come into this world?
   ◆ What does Jesus mean when he says, "I am the door (or gate)"?
   ◆ What does a good shepherd do (v. 11)?
   ◆ How is Jesus' identity as a door and good shepherd linked to his gift of abundant life?

2. Review the story of the widow at Zarephath in 1 Kings 17:1–16.
   ◆ When Elijah asked her for food, what do you think the widow was feeling? Have you ever felt that way?
   ◆ How much faith did it require to fulfill Elijah's request? What would you have done in her situation?
   ◆ Read the rest of the story in verses 17–24. What happened later in the narrative? What did Elijah do? How did the woman react? How do you imagine this event would affect the boy as he grew into adulthood?

CHAPTER FOUR QUESTIONS
A MATTER OF TRUST

Look Back

1. Jesus points to the birds, then poses the question: "Are you not much more valuable than they?"
   - With billions of humans in existence, do you ever question how God views you? Do you consider yourself to be "special"? Why or why not?
   - Cite evidence that God truly values you.
   - In the eyes of your Creator, does anything alter your intrinsic value?
   - Does God value others the same as you? Does their behavior (or anything else) affect their worth? How does your answer affect the way you interact with and treat people, especially those who are different from you?

2. Are you an anxiety expert? Do you fret about future uncertainties?
   - What do you tend to worry about most: health, appearance, relationships, money, the opinions others have about you, or something else?
   - On a scale of 1–10, what is your anxiety level today? What is at the top of your list of concerns right now?

3. The God who feeds finches and dresses dandelions knows your needs and won't ignore them.
   - Why do you suppose Jesus used birds and flowers to

illustrate his point? Is his teaching style effective for you?

- Instead of worrying about basic needs, what does Jesus say to focus on first (Matthew 6:33)? When do you struggle to follow this command? What will be the result of heeding his instructions?

4. Trust acknowledges that the God who made you and loves you will not forsake or abandon you, no matter how hopeless and helpless you feel.

- In John 6:35, Jesus says, "Whoever comes to me will never go hungry, and whoever believes in me will never be thirsty." What is the full meaning of this verse? How do these words comfort you?

- Jesus fed thousands by means of a miracle. Do you have to witness a miracle to have confidence in his promises? When your needs are taken care of in ordinary ways, does it diminish your appreciation of God's provision?

5. Little goes far when God is involved. Not enough becomes plenty. A shortage becomes excess. Lack becomes abundance. Faith small as a mustard seed moves a mountain. Don't you love knowing a morsel of trust outweighs Mount Everest?

- How important is faith when it comes to meeting your personal needs?

- Have you ever prayed for more faith? What are the dangerous and delightful ways God might answer that prayer?

6. What if you were anxious for nothing, including money? What

if you traded worrisome thoughts for unwavering trust? Instead of prioritizing your income statement, balance sheet, and retirement scenario, could seeking God's kingdom and righteousness be your first pursuits?

- What would your life be like if you worried less, trusted more, and committed daily to putting God's kingdom first?
- If you can trust God with your salvation, doesn't it make sense that you can trust him to provide for your essential needs?

Look Up

1. Read Psalm 139:13–16.
   - How involved was God in your formation?
   - What is the Psalmist's response in verse 14? Why?
   - Does God know the number of your days? Is this truth reassuring or troubling? How does this reality affect the way you think about the future?

2. Read Matthew 10:29–31.
   - Consider God's relationship with a sparrow. Contemplate the fact that God has numbered each hair on your head. What does it say about our Creator's involvement with his creation?
   - Why does Jesus say, "Don't be afraid"?

3. Read Matthew 7:9–12.
   - What happens when a person asks, seeks, and knocks? Do verses 7 and 8 guarantee God will fulfill every prayer exactly as it is requested? Explain your answer while contemplating your own personal experiences.

- Why does Jesus compare our parenting practices to that of our Father's? Does God want to give us good gifts?
- In verse 12, the celebrated "golden rule" closes this brief passage. Why does this moral law of reciprocity appear here?

CHAPTER FIVE QUESTIONS
A DIRE WARNING

Look Back

1. Jesus issued warnings. Some about hell. Some about false teaching. But he also cautioned us about greed. Paul lists greed alongside other sins improper for God's holy people: wickedness, depravity, evil, envy, sexual immorality, slander, impurity, idolatry, murder, and malice (Romans 1:29; 1 Corinthians 6:9–10; Ephesians 5:3).

    ◆ What does Jesus say about greed (Luke 12:15)? Why is he so concerned about material possessions? Is he exaggerating the danger just to make a point?

    ◆ Why does Paul put greed in the same category of sins as those listed above?

    ◆ Do you know any greedy people? What do you imagine their life is really like? Do you consider yourself—at least at times—to be a greedy person?

2. A priceless life—full of enjoyment, satisfaction, and purpose—cannot be purchased at a department store. No online store sells authentic joy. No indulgence brings lasting happiness. Yet billions of marketing dollars are spent annually trying to persuade you otherwise.

    ◆ What prompts you to make purchases beyond your actual needs? Is it pride, pleasure, power, or something else? Have you ever felt remorse after buying a big-ticket item? What's the most regrettable purchase you've ever made?

- What material possessions actually bring you happiness? How does that happiness compare with the joy of your closest relationships?

3. The kingdom of heaven is not Candyland. Deep in our hearts we want substance. Life that is truly life. And that comes only through loving, giving relationships with God and others.
   - In the parables of the hidden treasure and the pearl, both men sell everything to obtain something more valuable than what they had. Was it worth the trade?
   - What do you truly treasure in this life?

4. More toys. More clothes. More shoes. Bigger house. Built-in pool. Wider screen. Nicer car. Fatter paycheck. Season tickets. Speedboat. Getaway weekend. Exotic vacation. Tiffany jewelry. Coach purse. Second home. Third car. Four-wheeler. Five golden rings! When is enough, enough?
   - Do you have a finish line when it comes to finances and possessions? Or will you always want more, need more, and pursue more? For you, when is enough, enough?
   - Do you consider money or any of your possessions to be an idol? What would be your most difficult material item to give up?

5. We'd be wise to stop loving money and material goods. They'll never love us back. They don't last. And they're not coming with us when we die.
   - One minute after you die, who's going to control every dollar and doodad you now possess?

* Knowing that our stuff and money is so temporary, why do we still struggle with the desire to accumulate so much?

6. Like Jesus, Paul knew money-lovers would get into trouble. It comes with the territory.

* Jesus issues a one-or-the-other choice in Matthew 6:24: "You cannot serve both God and money." Why did he say this? Do you know anyone who has tried to serve both masters? Have you tried? What is the eventual result?
* Is money itself evil? What are some good things money can do?
* Why does Paul say that the love of money is a root of all kinds of evil? Describe some bad things that come from loving money.

Look Up

1. Read Proverbs 30:8–9.

* Of the three options presented in verse 8 (poverty, riches, or daily bread), what does the proverb writer request? Why? Does this make sense? Which would you choose?
* Have your unmet needs ever been so great that you've been tempted to steal?
* Are you wealthy enough now that you're financially self-sustaining? Do you run the risk of not needing the Lord for his daily provisions?
* Is one of your goals to become financially independent? What are the pros and cons of reaching that goal?

2. Read the following proverbs:

- "For the wicked boasts of the desires of his soul, and the one greedy for gain curses and renounces the Lord" (Psalm 10:3 ESV).
- "Such are the ways of everyone who is greedy for unjust gain; it takes away the life of its possessors" (Proverbs 1:19 ESV).
- "The greedy bring ruin to their households, but the one who hates bribes will live" (Proverbs 15:27).
- "The greedy stir up conflict, but those who trust in the Lord will prosper" (Proverbs 28:25).
- What do these verses teach us about greed?

CHAPTER SIX QUESTIONS
SOMETHING'S MISSING

Look Back

1. Humanity's first instance of deception was sown through seeds of discontentment. The familiar story takes place in a paradisical garden where sin is absent.
   - Envision the Garden of Eden before the fall. What appeals to you the most? The beauty? Perfection? Harmony? Lack of disease? Companionship with God?
   - What does the garden teach you about God?
   - Did Adam and Eve lack anything?

2. How did Satan lure Eve into sin? What did the devil do to provoke disobedience? The same thing he does today. Our adversary claims, "Something's missing." Something different. Something more. Something better.
   - When Satan said, "Did God really say . . ." he opened the door to doubting God. How else could Eve have responded in this situation? When have you doubted God? When have you stood strong in your faith?
   - How can you prevent yourself from doubting something God has already declared to be true?

3. Sins of pride fuel unhealthy comparison and ungodly competition. Our obsessed culture measures, ranks, grades, and counts. We sort, separate, select, and classify. We create top-to-bottom lists and categorization systems which create awareness of where we stand compared to our peers.

- Do you consider yourself a competitive person? If so, why do you think you're wired that way? How do you feel when you "win" or "lose" at anything?
- What are the dangers of incessant comparisons with other human beings? Do you believe God really cares where you rank on any given scale?
- Why did Teddy Roosevelt say, "Comparison is the thief of joy"? Do you agree or disagree?

4. *Maximizers* "seek and accept only the best." In contrast, a *satisficer* settles for good enough. Satisficers don't fret about the possibility that there might be something better out there.

- In general, are you a maximizer or satisficer? Give examples.
- What are the advantages and disadvantages of each disposition?

5. When a spirit of discontentment colonizes my mind, even God's powerful word has difficulty breaking through. Thorny soil rules the day. Worries of this life weigh me down. Deceitfulness of wealth sucks me in. Desire for other things sweeps me away. Nothing's actually missing, but I'm still searching.

- What are you still searching for? What do you still lack? If something is missing in your life, do you know what it is?
- Could it be that everything you really need is already in your possession? Could it be that you have much, much more than you actually need?

6. It's important to understand that contentment isn't synonymous with complacency. Nor is it an apathetic,

I-don't-care-about-anything attitude. There is a time to stay put and a time to saddle up.

- How do you decide when it's time to chase after something and time to rest in a state of contentment?
- When have you erred in judgment and pressed too hard or pursued the wrong goal? When have you sat idly or given up when you should have pressed forward?

7. Sufficient grace was part of Paul's secret to contentment. But even more so—the bigger picture—was the full measure of Christ himself.

- What is significant about Paul using the specific phrase we translate as "I have learned the secret of being content in any and every situation"? Reflect on the words "learned," "secret," and "any and every."
- Have you learned the secret? Explain your answer.

Look Up

1. Read Hebrews 13:5.

- What is the clear instruction given?
- What promise motivates us to follow this directive?
- How does this promise affect your level of contentment?

2. Read 1 Timothy 6:6–7.

- Fill in the blank: Godliness with _____ is great gain (v. 6).
- According to verse 7, what did we bring into this world? What can we take out of it?
- How does this change your view of possessions?

CHAPTER SEVEN QUESTIONS
THREE WORDS

Look Back

1. It's not the quantity of words that matter, it's the sincerity with which we say them. "Thank you" conveys the sentiment; "Lord" indicates to whom we're giving thanks.
   - How often do these three words spring off your tongue?
   - When are you most likely to say them?

2. It's one thing to have thoughts of thanks and another to tangibly express them. If you feel something, say something. When we thank God, we praise God.
   - Have you ever had an experience similar to that of the healed lepers? Describe it.
   - How would you feel if you gave a precious gift to someone and they never thanked you for it? Has that ever happened?
   - Why are thanks and praise so closely related?

3. The Bible tells us to be thankful in *all* circumstances, not just when we're delivered from dread. For "this is God's will for you in Christ Jesus" (1 Thessalonians 5:18).
   - Why are we instructed to always be giving thanks? Why is this God's will?
   - Can you recall a time you expressed thanks for an unwanted or painful experience? Did giving thanks affect your perspective of the situation?

4. Don't overlook the source of your blessings. Lucky stars have

nothing to do with them. Good fortune hasn't singled you out. Every good gift comes from the Giver.

* Name some of the things God has given you.
* Try to name any good thing you have that did not come from God. Can you do it?
* How does the knowledge that God is the giver of all good things affect your desire to be generous?

5. You can't overestimate the power of gratitude. Some deem it the healthiest of all human emotions. Roman philosopher Cicero believed gratitude to be not only the greatest of virtues but the parent of all others.

* Do you agree with Cicero? Why does he put gratitude at the top of the virtue list?
* What are some physical benefits of gratitude? What are some emotional and spiritual benefits?
* Do you notice a difference in your well-being when you have a grateful attitude? Does it affect your mood? Your relationships? Your work? Your stress level?
* Do others notice when you're feeling and acting grateful?

6. In the children's classic *Winnie-the-Pooh*, one line A. A. Milne penned convicts me: "Piglet noticed that even though he had a Very Small Heart, it could hold a rather large amount of Gratitude."

* How much gratitude does *your* heart hold? How do you keep your heart full?
* Do you have any habits or practices that help you maintain a spirit of gratitude? Have you considered keeping a gratitude journal?

♦ What big things and little things are you grateful for today?

Look Up

1. Read Psalm 136:1–26.

   ♦ What stands out to you in this passage?

   ♦ Did you notice how it opens and closes? How many times do the words "give thanks" appear?

   ♦ What are some of God's mighty acts cited in this psalm?

   ♦ What phrase is repeated twenty-six times? Why do you think the author chooses this refrain? How thankful are you that God's indescribable love lasts forever?

   ♦ Try to write a personalized psalm using the format of Psalm 136. Be sure to list God's activity in your own life.

2. Read Colossians 3:15–17.

   ♦ What should we allow to rule in our hearts (v. 15)? What else does verse 15 say?

   ♦ What should dwell in us richly (v. 16)? And what should be in our hearts as we sing?

   ♦ What does verse 17 tell us to do? How does that verse end?

CHAPTER EIGHT QUESTIONS
IT'S GOING TO COST YOU

Look Back

1. When did you last feel the joy of giving a costly gift?
   - Have you had second thoughts about making that gift?
   - Besides joy, what other emotions did you feel? Fear? Remorse? Satisfaction? Love? Gratitude? Hope? A sense of purpose?
   - Was the gift so costly that someone questioned your judgment? What did they say?

2. When we give our prized possessions (like Chas), or a vital organ (like Melissa), it comes at a price. But the cost of generosity is never higher than the cost of following Christ.
   - How do the stories of Chas and Melissa inspire you?
   - Does it make logical sense that the cost of generosity is never higher than the cost of following Christ? Why or why not? What have you given up in order to follow Christ?

3. God requires the first and best of all you have and all you are. Second place won't do. Leftovers don't cut it. Afterthoughts aren't acceptable. There's no negotiating this everlasting point. With the first commandment, the royal magistrate strikes his gavel: "You shall have no other gods before me" (Exodus 20:3).
   - Why does God start his list of commandments with this one?
   - What other "gods" are competing for your attention right now?

- What consistent, practical actions do you take to keep God first in your life?

4. If becoming a "living sacrifice" sounds extreme, take comfort: "There is no spiritual path more secure than that of giving yourself entirely to God."
   - What does it mean to become a "living sacrifice"?
   - When you completely surrender to God, do you feel a sense of security? Why or why not?

5. Authentic faith triggers eccentric behavior.
   - Who have you seen model authentic faith?
   - What radical examples of faith have you witnessed?
   - On a scale of 1–10, how would you rate the strength of your faith? Thinking back, at what point in life was your faith at its peak? How does your faith affect your behavior? Your mood? Your peace? Your giving?

6. What's your obstacle? The barrier standing between you and Jesus?
   - Is it related to money, a relationship, status, a besetting sin, or something else?
   - How can this barrier be broken?

7. Would you give up something as common as money so that *others* might gain entrance into heaven?
   - What types of ministries and needs do you enjoy giving to?
   - When did you last make a gift as a sacrifice of thanksgiving?
   - Does the thought of sacrificial generosity stir up feelings of anxiety and distress, exuberant joy, or some other mix of emotions?

+ Has God prompted you to consider making a sacrificial gift in the near future?

Look Up

1. Read 2 Corinthians 8:2–8.
   + How much did the Macedonian Christians give (v. 3)? What prompted their generosity (v. 2)? Did they have to be asked to give (v. 3–4)?
   + Verse 4 says they gave themselves first to the Lord. Why is that important?
   + What does Paul say about the grace of giving in verse 7? Why does he say this (v. 8)?
   + Continue reading 2 Corinthians 8:9–15. What do verses 12–15 tell us about motivation, amount, and reciprocity?

2. Read Mark 12:41–44.
   + Why do you think Jesus was watching people put their money in the temple treasury (v. 41)?
   + What were many rich people doing (v. 41)? What did the poor widow do (v. 42)?
   + Apparently, this teaching opportunity was so vital, verse 43 notes Jesus called his disciples to him to drive home a point. Does this detail change anything about the way you view this story?

CHAPTER NINE QUESTIONS
BRUSHSTROKES

Look Back

1. Jesus tells a parable illustrating how to love your neighbor, reminding us that love gives. But love doesn't just give money. Love is, after all, mostly *not* about the transfer of material possessions.

   ◆ What are the different ways the Good Samaritan expressed love to the stranger he encountered?

   ◆ Have you, like the innkeeper, witnessed a Good Samaritan in action? When have you acted like one yourself? When have you acted more like the priest or Levite in this story?

2. Generosity, the manifestation of *love-that-gives*, involves so much more than financial transactions. Generosity incorporates all resources at your disposal—money, time, abilities, and going-the-extra-mile energy—as well as the palette of your emotions, especially compassion.

   ◆ Is it common to associate generosity nearly exclusively with money? If so, why is this the case?

   ◆ Why should generosity include all resources at your disposal? Is this a new way of thinking for you?

3. How might your diverse expressions—your brushstrokes of generosity—transform lives? Would they make the world a better place?

   ◆ Describe a time when someone was especially generous toward you. How did it make you feel?

- When was the last time one of your brushstrokes of generosity made a difference in the life of someone else? Was it a simple act of kindness or a significant sacrifice? What did it feel like?

- Thinking about your own generosity, complete this sentence: If everyone exhibited the same level of generosity I do, the world would _____.

4. BE GENEROUS WITH YOUR MONEY AND MATERIAL POSSESSIONS.

- How generous are you with your money and material possessions? Are you satisfied with the percentage of income you give away to church, charity, and people in need? If someone asked to borrow one of your cherished possessions, how would you respond?

- Who do you know personally who serves as a good role model in this area?

- What is the next step you can take to grow in your financial giving? When will you do it?

5. BE GENEROUS WITH YOUR TIME.

- How generous are you with your time? How many hours per month do you volunteer for worthy causes? How available are you to serve others? Are you too busy to help those who need you?

- Who do you know personally who serves as a good role model in this area?

- What is the next step you can take to become more generous with your time? When will you do it?

6. BE GENEROUS WITH YOUR TALENTS, ABILITIES, AND GIFTS.

  - How generous are you with your talents, abilities, and gifts? Which of these assets do you regularly employ to serve others? Do you feel joy when you use your unique gifts to serve God and others?
  - Who do you know personally who serves as a good role model in this area?
  - What is the next step you can take to become more generous with your talents, abilities, and gifts? When will you do it?

7. BE GENEROUS TO YOUR SPOUSE, FAMILY, FRIENDS, THE NEEDY, AND THOSE WHO SEEMINGLY DON'T DESERVE IT.

  - Typically, who is the beneficiary of your generous acts?
  - Would the people closest to you say you're extravagantly generous to them? What are some ways you can show them kindness?
  - How often do you go out of your way to be generous toward strangers, enemies, and those you don't think deserve it?

Look Up

1. Read Ephesians 2:4–10.
  - When did God make us alive in Christ (v. 5)? Why did he do this (v. 4)?
  - What do verses 7–8 tell us about God's grace and how it is expressed?
  - What does verse 10 say we were created to do? Does this

knowledge motivate you to make any changes in your life?

- Do you ever feel inadequate, uncomfortable, or unworthy to do good works? If so, how can you shift to a more eager, enthusiastic, and confident mindset?

2. Read Romans 12:4–13; 1 Corinthians 12:12–31; Ephesians 4:11–13; and 1 Peter 4:10–11.
   - What stands out to you in these passages?
   - What reasons are cited for using the gifts God has given us?
   - Name some adjectives and adverbs listed indicating how we are to deploy our gifts.
   - Are there any exemptions or exceptions for people who are too busy to engage or simply don't feel like serving, giving, or loving others?

CHAPTER TEN QUESTIONS
PRICELESS

Look Back

1. Have you ever experienced a eureka moment? A sudden flash of insight or golden revelation?
   - Was it spiritual in nature, or something else?
   - Have you noticed a connection between happiness and generosity? In others or yourself?
   - When you reflect on instances when you've been extravagantly generous, what emotions are evoked?

2. The *best* things money can't buy come from Jesus. In the truest sense of the word, what Jesus did for you is priceless.
   - Of the examples listed in this chapter, which one(s) resonate with you most right now? Has that changed over time?
   - Do you ever feel unworthy of the generous gifts Jesus offers?
   - How might Jesus' actions spur you on toward greater generosity?

3. I take great comfort knowing God's love orbits every atom in my body like swirling electrons. But I'm acutely aware I am not the only one he loves.
   - Rate your ability to feel empathy on a scale of 1–10. How well do you relate to people who don't look like you, think like you, or act like you?

- When you encounter someone with opposing religious, social, or political views, how does that affect your view of that person? Is there a small part of you that thinks they might not be as priceless to Jesus as you are?

4. The revelation—you're far happier giving than getting—is merely a spiritual paradox, not unlike others Jesus shares that flip our world upside down.
   - Do you fully believe the statement, "It is more blessed to give than to receive"? Why or why not? When have you seen or personally experienced the truth of these words?
   - Why does Jesus say, "Whoever wants to be great among you must become a servant" (Matthew 20:26)?
   - Why does Jesus say, "Whoever finds his life will lose it, and whoever loses his life for my sake will find it" (Matthew 10:39)?

5. There are hundreds of biblical "*so that*" statements which explain the reason *for* or result *of* a particular situation or action. A few questions to consider . . .
   - Why does God help you stand steady and strong (1 Corinthians 1:8)?
   - Why does God embrace us with compassion in times of need (2 Corinthians 1:4)?
   - Why does God bless you above and beyond what anyone deserves (2 Corinthians 9:8)?
   - Why does God give you the ability to (among other things) earn income and accumulate wealth (2 Corinthians 9:11)?

6. What do *you* do when you feel unable, unwilling, or unmotivated to be generous?
   - Are you still growing in your faith, learning to trust your provider?
   - Will you resolve to live the life of purpose and meaning to which you've been called?
   - Name some of the truths covered in the book that can help you move forward on your generosity journey.

7. What do people want most out of life?
   - What do *you* want most out of life?
   - What is the secret to living a priceless life?
   - Do you intend to share this secret with others?

Look Up

1. Psalm 36:7 says, "How priceless is your unfailing love, O God!"
   - Why does the Psalmist use a word we translate into English as "priceless" (or "precious")?
   - What are some other words you might use to describe God's love?
   - How has God expressed his priceless love to you personally?

2. Read Psalm 139:1–4.
   - What does this passage say about how much God is paying attention to you?
   - Do you think he is aware of your struggles and victories in the area of giving?
   - Do you believe he wants to help you grow on your happily generous journey?

3. Read Philippians 2:13–14; Hebrews 12:1; and 1 Timothy 4:7–8.

 * Now that you've finished this book, how do these verses
   encourage you to commit to follow through on whatever
   God is leading you to do?

ACKNOWLEDGMENTS

How fitting is this reality: Without the inspiring generosity of companions that helped me, this book would not exist. From start to finish, I've been surrounded by a team of cheerleaders, coaches, sherpas, and, when necessary, energetic drill sergeants. For their unwavering support and encouragement, I am forever grateful. Thank you, Lord, for them.

My wife, Mary Ann—I felt it in my soul, we were meant to be. Bob Seger sang *You'll Accomp'ny Me* just for us. Thanks for forty-two years of "someday."

Our children, Michele, Melanie, Melissa, and Matthew—Next to mom, you four are my greatest blessing. "Don't you see that children are God's best gift?" (Psalm 127:3 THE MESSAGE). Oh yes, I see.

Mom—You always believed in me. You know why you were born. So do I.

Dad—You taught me to work hard, value others, and love my family.

My siblings, Cathi, Laura, Johnny, and Theresa—God assembled us together for a reason. Thank you for continuing to model generosity like our mother.

Holly Kammier, Jessica Hammett, and the team at Acorn Publish-

ing—When I hit the wall in this uphill marathon, you carried me over the finish line. May a grove of mighty oak trees be planted in your honor.

My cherished friend and favorite author Mark Atteberry—Could this book have been written without your never-ending encouragement? Not a chance. I felt the wind of your kind words always at my back.

Darren Key—God knew what he was doing when he matched us together in ministry. Thanks for your friendship, and for spurring me on to write this book.

Melinda Rutland—You buffed and polished my manuscript as if it were a Rolls Royce headed to the showroom floor.

My generous friends who read the first draft of this manuscript. Melissa Chappell, Michele Muscarella, Malcolm Puckett, Rob Pease, Kevin Ingram, Joe Putting, Roger Shepherd, Pat Williams, David McGrew, Alan Ahlgrim, Mike Waers, Eddie Lowen, Leo Sabo, Jeff Sharda, Clay Perkins, Greg Lindsey, Stephen Waers, Johnna Reeder Kleymeyer, Phil Ayres, Tom Milajecki, and to the others I'm forgetting right now, grant me grace. To each of you I award five kindness stars and 1,000 generosity points.

And of course, *Thank you, Lord*, our Great Giver and Generous One. The kingdom, power, and glory are yours. Forever.

ABOUT THE AUTHOR

Mike Kocolowski serves as Chief Stewardship Officer at Christian Financial Resources (CFR), a nonprofit ministry committed to "funding ministry, changing lives." He holds degrees from the University of South Florida (B.S. Business Administration) and Reformed Theological Seminary (M. A. Theological Studies) and has completed coursework toward his Ph.D. at the Regent University School of Global Leadership & Entrepreneurship. Additionally, he has earned the CFRE (Certified Fundraising Executive) credential from CFRE International.

Mike and his high school sweetheart, Mary Ann, reside in the countryside near Orlando, Florida. They have four children, five grandchildren, and a herd of friendly farm animals. Mike loves time with family, playing golf, watching sports, and traveling. He also enjoys building things, solving puzzles, and walking at least 10,000 steps a day.

Mike would love to hear from you. You can reach him at: mikekocolowski@outlook.com.

NOTES

Introduction: More Blessed

1. Henri Nouwen, *Life of the Beloved* (New York, NY: Crossroad Publishing Company, 1992), 106.

Chapter One: The Great Giver

1. John Piper, *Desiring God* (Colorado Springs, CO: Multnomah, 2011), 32.

2. Bruce K. Waltke, *Genesis: A Commentary* (Grand Rapids, MI: Zondervan, 2001), 59.

3. Brennan Manning, *The Raggamuffin Gospel* (Sisters, OR: Multnomah, 2005), 14.

Chapter Two: Born For This

1. Traditionally, Solomon is regarded as the author of Ecclesiastes, but not all scholars agree.

2. James Hollis, PhD, *What Matters Most: Living a More Considered Life* (New York, NY: Gotham Books, 2009), xv.

3. Rich Mullins, "My One Thing" *Songs*, Reunion Records, Inc. 1996.

4. Bruce K. Waltke, *An Old Testament Theology* (Grand Rapids, MI: Zondervan, 2007), 964.

5. Michael A. Eaton, *Ecclesiastes: An Introduction and Commentary, The Tyndale Old Testament Commentaries 18* (Downers Grove, IL: Intervarsity Press), 48.

6. G. I. Williamson, *The Westminster Shorter Catechism 2nd Edition* (Phillipsburg, NJ: P&R, 1970), 1.

7. Matthew 5:16.

8. Shel Silverstein, *The Giving Tree* (HarperCollins Publishers: New York, NY, 1964), no page numbers.

Chapter Three: What Holds You Back?

1. Christian Smith, Michael O. Emerson, *Passing the Plate: Why American Christians Don't Give Away More Money* (Oxford, NY: Oxford University Press, 2008), 3.

2. Leonardo Blair, "Only 13% of Evangelicals Tithe, Half Give Away Less Than 1% of Income Annually: Study," *The Christian Post*, October 29, 2021, https://www.christianpost.com/news/only-13-of-evangelicals-tithe-study.html.

3. "Evangelicals and Giving," Grey Matter Research, November 6, 2021, https://greymatterresearch.com/evangelicals-and-giving/.

4. Proverbs 3:9.

5. Luke 6:38.

6. Christian Smith, Hilary Davidson, *The Paradox of Generosity* (Oxford, NY, Oxford University Press: 2014), 11.

7. Christian Smith, Michael O. Emerson, *Passing the Plate*, 178.

8. Lynne Twist, *The Soul of Money* (New York, NY: W.W. Norton, 2017), 49.

9. Steven Spielberg, John Williams, John Williams & John Neufeld. (1993) *Schindler's List*. USA.

10. "How Rich Am I?" *Giving What We Can*, accessed June 21, 2022, http://tinyurl.com/4h9ravsy.

11. Delta Seat Maps, *Seat Gurus by TripAdvisor*, accessed June 22, 2022, Note: there are 28 closed suites (first class) on this jet and 296 seats overall. https://www.seatguru.com/airlines/Delta_Airlines/Delta_Airlines_Boeing_777-200ER_V2.php.

12. Anshool Deshmukh, "This Simple Chart Reveals the Distribution of Global Wealth," *Visual Capitalist*, September 20, 2021, https://www. visualcapitalist.com/distribution-of-global-wealth-chart/.

13. "World Hunger Facts," *Action Against Hunger*, accessed June 25, 2022, https://www.actionagainsthunger.org/world-hunger-facts-statistics.

14. Graeme Wood, "Secret Fears of the Super-Rich," *The Atlantic*, April 2011, https://www.theatlantic.com/magazine/archive/2011/04/secret-fears-of-the-super-rich/308419/.

15. *Life Without Lack* is the title to a book by Dallas Willard.

Chapter Four: A Matter of Trust

1. "£12,000 portrait revealed to be a £100m Leonardo after art detectives discover the master's fingerprint," *The Daily Mail*, October 13, 2009, accessed December 23, 2023, https://www.dailymail.co.uk/news/article-1219988/New-Leonardo-da-Vinci-portrait-discovered-matched-artists-fingerprint.html.

2. David Grann, "The Mark of a Masterpiece," The New Yorker, July 5, 2010, https://www.newyorker.com/magazine/2010/07/12/the-mark-of-a-masterpiece.

3. La Bella Principessa. (2022, October 10). In Wikipedia. https://en.wikipedia.org/wiki/La_Bella_Principessa.

4. Psalm 139:14.

5. "Luke Aikins. (2022, October 14). In *Wikipedia*. https://en.wikipedia.org/wiki/Luke_Aikins.

6. "Skydiver Luke Aikins makes parachute-free jump," *CBS News Los Angeles*, July 30, 2016, https://www.cbsnews.com/news/skydiver-luke-aikins-makes-parachute-free-jump/.

Chapter Five: A Dire Warning

1. "21 Stupid Warning Labels That Will Make You Feel Like a Genius," *Reader's Digest*, November 29, 2021, accessed October 26, 2022, https://www.rd.com/list/funny-warning-labels/.

2. Dallas Willard, *Life Without Lack* (Nashville, TN: Thomas Nelson, 2019), 134.

3. "Body of Lottery Winner Found Buried in Florida," *BBC News*, January 30, 2010, accessed December 23, 2022, http://news.bbc.co.uk/2/hi/americas/8489582.stm.

4. Ibid.

5. Gina Martinez, "Everything You Know About the Fate of Lottery Winners Is Probably Wrong, According to Science," *Time*, October 18, 2018, https://time.com/5427275/lottery-winning-happiness-debunked/.

6. Arthur Brooks, "How to Identify What You Enjoy," *Podcast: How to Build a Happy Life: Episode 11/23/2021*. Mr. Brooks uses these three words in this order to describe happiness.

7. "How Much Would it Cost to End World Hunger," March 8, 2022, http://tinyurl.com/5a6e4e8z. A study in Germany suggests $330B spent over 10 years would end world hunger.

   A. Gutman, *Global Advertising Spending 2000-2024*, September 16, 2022, https://www.statista.com/statistics/1174981/advertising-expenditure-worldwide/. Note: In 2022, advertising spending is estimated to be over $781B, and will continue to rise in coming years.

8. Daniel Barbarisi, "The Man Who Found Forest Fenn's Treasure," December 7, 2020, https://www.outsideonline.com/outdoor-adventure/exploration-survival/forrest-fenn-treasure-jack-stuef/.

9. "One Chest of Gold, Five Deaths: The Search for Forrest Fenn's Treasure," *CBS News*, December 25, 2021, https://www.cbsnews.com/news/forrest-fenn-treasure-five-deaths-48-hours/.

10. Salama Yusuf, "Are Diamonds Really Forever?" March 11, 2011, https://www.scienceabc.com/eyeopeners/are-diamonds-really-forever.html.

Chapter Six: Something's Missing

1. Barry Schwartz, *The Paradox of Choice* (New York, NY: Harper Collins, 2004, 2016), 79.

2. David Goggins, *Can't Hurt Me* (Carson City, NV: Lioncrest, 2020). The phrase "colonizes your mind" is mentioned in the audible version of this book.

3. This is how Russell Conwell concluded his speech. Mike Brunel, "Are There Acres of Diamonds in your Backyard?" March 20, 2019, https://www.mikebrunel.com/diamonds-in-your-backyard/.

Chapter Seven: Three Words

1. "Gettysburg Address: 1863" Ben's Guide, January 8, 2024, http://tinyurl.com/497ephwh.

2. Christina Sterzbenz, "Lincoln's Gettysburg Address Totally Overshadowed This Guy's Two-Hour Speech At The Same Event," Edward Everett Also Spoke at Gettysburg Convention (businessinsider.com), November 19, 2013.

3. "Letter To Edward Everett," Abraham Lincoln Online, 2020, https://www.abrahamlincolnonline.org/lincoln/speeches/everett.htm.

4. Dr. Alan L. Gillen, "Biblical Leprosy: Shedding Light on the Disease that Shuns," June 10, 2007; last featured October 25, 2009 in *Answers Magazine*, https://answersingenesis.org/biology/disease/biblical-leprosy-shedding-light-on-the-disease-that-shuns/.

5. Andrzej Grzybowski MD, PhD and Malgorzata Nita MD, PhD, "Leprosy in the Bible," *Clinics in Dermatology: Vol 34., Issue 1*, January-February 2016 pages 3–7, accessed March 10, 2023, https://www.sciencedirect.com/science/article/abs/pii/S0738081X15001820.

6. R.C. Sproul, Cleansing of the Leper, Nov. 9, 2014, Sermon form the Lord's Day pulpit ministry of R.C. Sproul at Saint Andrews Chapel, Sanford Florida, https://www.ligonier.org/learn/sermons/cleansing-leper-luke.

7. William Law, edited by Dave Hunt, *The Power of the Spirit* (USA: CLC Publications, 1971), 21.

8. Henri Nouwen, *Turn My Mourning Into Dancing: Finding Hope in Hard Times* (Nashville, TN: Thomas Nelson Publishing, 2004), 17.

9. Oliver Sacks, *Gratitude*, (New York, NY: Knoph, 2015), 20.

10. Lisa Sink, PGA video shown during interview of Stewart Sink at Fairway Christian Church in The Villages, FL, March 13, 2023.

11. Randy Alcorn, *Happiness*, (Carol Stream, IL: Tyndale House Publishers, 2015), 19.

12. This is the number often cited by Bible researchers and scholars. See
the following:
https://www.envoyfinancial.com/participantresources/bible-verses-
about-money-and-stewardship#:~:text=Did%20you%20know%20
that%20there,related%20to%20money%20and%20possessions

https://churchleaders.com/outreach-missions/outreach-missions-
articles/314227-2350-bible-verses-money.html.

Gregory Baumer & John Cortines, God and Money: How We
Discovered True Riches at Harvard Business School (Carson, CA,
Rose Publishing: 2016), 13.

13. Nancy DeMoss Wolgemuth, *Choosing Gratitude*, (Chicago, Il,
Moody: 2009, 2021), 36.

14. C.S. Lewis, *A Grief Observed*, (New York, NY, Harper Collins:
1961), 1

15. Nancy DeMoss Wolgemuth, *Choosing Gratitude*, (Chicago, Il,
Moody: 2009, 2021), 12.

16. Quote attributed to Zig Ziglar.
https://www.ziglar.com/articles/the-gratitude-journey/.

17. Sonja Lyubomirsky, *The How of Happiness*, (New York, NY:
Penguin Books, 2007), 89.

18. Ibid, 94.

19. Mayo Clinic Health System, "Can Expressing Gratitude Improve
Your Mental, Physical Health?" December 6, 2022,
https://www.mayoclinichealthsystem.org/hometown-
health/speaking-of-health/can-expressing-gratitude-improve-
health.

20. Madhuleena Roy Chowdhury, BA, reviewed by William Smith,
Ph.D., "The Neuroscience of Gratitude and Effects on the Brain,"
Positive Psychology, April 9, 2019. http://tinyurl.com/bdywja54.

21. I've seen this quote in several places but cannot confirm the original
author.

Chapter Eight: It's Going to Cost You

1. Jordan Bowen, "Man sells valuable possessions to help church," Fox 13 News, November 18, 2019, https://www.fox13news.com/news/man-sells-valuable-possessions-to-help-church.

2. "Newlyweds' Valentine's Day Kidney Transplant a Success," News 13 Florida, Seminole County, February 14, 2013, https://www.baynews9.com/fl/tampa/news/2013/2/8/kidney_for_valentine.

3. Jean-Pierre de Caussade, *The Joy of Full Surrender*, (Brewster, MA: Paraclete Press, 2008), front cover.

4. Ibid, back cover.

5. J.R. Miller, "At the Feet of Jesus: A Talk to Christian Young Women," 1891, https://www.gracegems.org/Miller/at_the_feet_of_jesus.htm.

6. Tim Burton, (2005). Charlie and the Chocolate Factory. Warner Bros. Words from a scene in the movie.

Chapter Nine: Brushstrokes

1. "Road to Jericho (Setting for the Good Samaritan)" University of Notre Dame, https://faith.nd.edu/s/1210/faith/interior.aspx?sid=1210&gid=609&pgid=33100

2. "A Good Samaritan Breaks the Rules," https://www.jesus-story.net/the-good-samaritan/.

3. Don Stewart, "Who Were the Samaritans?" *Blue Letter Bible*, accessed December 25, 2023, https://www.blueletterbible.org/faq/don_stewart/don_stewart_1319.cfm.

4. Mimi Leder, (2000). Pay It Forward. Warner Bros.

5. Thomas Cahill, *Desire of the Everlasting Hills: The World Before and After Jesus (The Hinges of History, Vol. III)*, (New York, NY: Anchor, 2001), 185.

6. Luke 19:8.

7. Matthew 27:57-60.

8. Acts 4:36-37.

9. John 6:9.

10. Charles Spurgeon, "19 Spurgeon Quotes for Coping with Stress and Anxiety," October 6, 2016. https://www.spurgeon.org/resource-library/blog-entries/19-spurgeon-quotes-for-coping-with-stress-and-anxiety/

11. Adam Grant, *Give and Take* (New York, NY: Penguin Group, 2013), 55.

12. John Piper, "Don't Waste Your Life" Seven Minutes That Moved a Generation. Message excerpt, May 19, 2017, https://www.desiringgod.org/messages/boasting-only-in-the-cross/excerpts/dont-waste-your-life.

13. Adam Grant, *Give and Take* (New York, NY: Penguin Group, 2013), 45.

Chapter Ten: Priceless

1. Raja Rajamannar, *Marking 25 Years of Priceless*, October 25, 2022, https://www.mastercard.com/news/perspectives/2022/priceless-25-year-anniversary/.

2. White Mountain Puzzles, https://www.whitemountainpuzzles.com/pages/train-your-brain.

3. The phrase "so that" appears over 700 times in the NIV. Bible Gateway search, accessed December 26, 2023. https://www.biblegateway.com/quicksearch/?quicksearch=%22so+that%22&version=NIV

4. Anne Marshall, One Happy Place! "Art & Science of Happiness: 10 Things We All Want in Life," April, 19, 2019, https://onehappyplace.org/10-things-we-all-want-in-life/.

5. Arthur Brooks, The Atlantic "Three Myths and Four Truths About How to Get Happier," quoting St. Augustine in 426 C.E, September, 12, 2023, https://www.theatlantic.com/ideas/archive/2023/09/happiness-truths-myths/675283/.